Music Theory in Practice

Grade 6

PETER ASTON & JULIAN WEBB

The Associated Board of the Royal Schools of Music

Syllabus for Grade 6

As in preceding grades. The harmonic vocabulary expected will include: the use of $\frac{5}{3}$, $\frac{6}{3}$ and $\frac{6}{4}$ chords on any degree of the major or minor (harmonic and melodic) scale; the recognition of the dominant 7th chord in root position, first, second and third inversions, and the supertonic 7th chord in root position and first inversion, in any major or minor key; and the figuring for all these chords. An understanding of the principles of modulation and a knowledge of cadences, ornamentation and melodic decoration (which might include passing notes, auxiliary notes, appoggiaturas, changing notes and notes of anticipation) will also be expected. Questions will cover:

(1) Writing specified chords for voices in four parts *or* for keyboard (at the candidate's choice) above a given bass part of about four bars.

(2) The indication of suitable chords for the accompaniment of a diatonic melody of about eight bars in any key, using any recognised method of notation, *or* (at the candidate's choice) the provision of a bass to a given melody, adding figures to indicate the intended harmonies.

(3) Composition of a melody for a specified instrument (a choice will be given), using a given opening. Modulation to the dominant, subdominant, relative major or relative minor may be required.

(4) Questions on short extracts of music written for piano or in open score for voices or for any combination of instruments and/or voices, designed to test the candidate's knowledge of the elements and notation of music, including the realisation of ornaments, the identification and notation of underlying harmonic structure, phrase structure, style, performance, and on the voices and instruments for which the works were written.

First published in 1992 by
The Associated Board of the Royal Schools of Music (Publishing) Ltd

Reprinted in 1993, 1994 (with revisions) and 2000

© 1992 by The Associated Board of the Royal Schools of Music

ISBN I 85472 591 2

Typesetting and music processing by Halstan & Co. Ltd, Amersham, Bucks
Printed in Great Britain by Headley Brothers Ltd, Ashford, Kent

Contents

Thanks are due to the following for permission to reprint extracts
from copyright works: Boosey & Hawkes Music Publishers Ltd;
Faber Music Ltd; Novello & Co. Ltd; Oxford University Press;
G. Ricordi & C.s.p.a.

The music on the cover is the opening of an arrangement
for trumpet in D and piano by Philip Cranmer of the aria,
'The trumpet shall sound', from Handel's *Messiah*
(*Handel and Bach Arias*, published by the Associated Board).

In the quoted music examples, tempo marks and dynamics without brackets
occur in the original as shown, while those enclosed in square brackets
are editorial. Tempo marks occurring earlier in the music are enclosed in
round brackets.

Students should use their own manuscript paper for Exercises 4–7. All
other exercises should be worked in the book.

A Realising figured basses

(See *The AB Guide to Music Theory*, Part I, 8/4)

Figured bass is a method of shorthand for indicating chords. It was used widely during the 17th and 18th centuries; and although you will rarely see figuring in music from later periods (an exception is jazz notation in which letter names are sometimes combined with figuring), it continues to be a useful way of describing harmonies[1].

In Grade 6, knowledge of the figuring for all chords in the syllabus is required, and it will be tested by a question in which you are asked to realise (i.e. write chords above) a figured-bass part. You will be given the choice of laying out the chords for four-part voices (SATB) or for keyboard. Because the bass is figured, you do not have to work out a suitable harmonic progression: the chords to be used are all shown. The exercises at the end of this section, and similar ones in the examination papers, test your ability:

(a) to recognise which chords are indicated by the figuring, and
(b) to lay out these chords effectively for your chosen medium – voices or keyboard.

The chords which may be used in Grade 6 are $\frac{5}{3}$, $\frac{6}{3}$, $\frac{6}{4}$, $\frac{7}{5}$, $\frac{6}{5}$, $\frac{6}{4}$ and $\frac{6}{2}$. Because it is cumbersome to write out these chords in full, they are usually abbreviated as follows:

no figuring = $\frac{5}{3}$ 7 = $\frac{7}{5}$ 6 = $\frac{6}{3}$ $\frac{6}{5}$ = $\frac{6}{5}$ $\frac{4}{3}$ = $\frac{6}{4}$ $\frac{4}{2}$ = $\frac{6}{4}$

Note that one chord, the $\frac{6}{4}$, is always figured in full. This is to distinguish it from 6 (= $\frac{6}{3}$), and a common mistake made by beginners is to confuse these two chords. Notice the difference between Ex.1a (a progression rarely used in Baroque music) and Ex.1b.

EXAMPLE 1a   1b

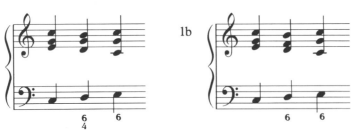

It is important to remember that figures refer to diatonic intervals above the given bass note in accordance with the given key signature. Thus, with a key signature of two flats, a 6 above the note G would be E♭. If the composer wanted E♮, he would have to show this in the figuring by placing a natural sign next to the figure 6.[2] Similarly, with the same key signature of two flats, a 4 above the note C is F♮. If the composer wanted F♯, as he might in the key of G minor, he would place a sharp sign next to the 4.[3] Note that an accidental appearing on its own always refers to the third above the bass note, so ♯ = 3♯ (implying $\frac{5}{3♯}$),

---

[1]Unlike the Roman numeral system, however, figured bass does not show the harmonic function of chords and therefore cannot be used for harmonic analysis, unless the figuring is accompanied by an explanation of how each chord is related to the key of the passage in which it occurs.

[2]A chromatic alteration may be placed before or after the figure to which it applies.

[3]Another method of showing that a note is to be raised by a semitone is to cross the numeral with a stroke. Thus, with a key signature of two flats, 6♮ above G (= E♮) could be written as 6̸, and 4♯ above C (= F♯) could be written as 4+. You will often see the crossed-numeral symbol in printed scores, but in the examination tests any chromatic raising of a note will always be shown by an accidental placed next to the numeral. Note that there is no symbol for showing the chromatic lowering of a note other than placing the appropriate accidental beside the numeral (e.g. 7♭, cancelling a natural in the key signature, or 7♮, cancelling a sharp).

and $\frac{6}{4} = \frac{6}{3\natural}$. The following passage includes most of the chromatic alterations you are likely to find in Grade 6.

EXAMPLE 2

Unless the music modulates (i.e. moves to or passes through a new key), chromatic alterations to chords in the Grade 6 syllabus will occur only when the passage is in a minor key. The chords most likely to be affected are the tonic (which is sometimes changed to a major chord at the final cadence) and the dominant and subdominant chords which can be major or minor depending upon their context. In Ex.3, both forms of the tonic, subdominant and dominant chords are used.

EXAMPLE 3

The supertonic chord may also contain a chromatic alteration, in this case to the 5.
In the key of C minor, for example, a $\frac{5}{3}$ on the supertonic consists of the notes F and A♭ above the bass note D, but in the ascending melodic minor scale the diminished 5th (A♭) is raised to A♮. Both forms of the supertonic chord are used in Ex.4.

EXAMPLE 4

One other commonly used symbol may be found in the examination tests. This is the horizontal dash, indicating that the chord used above the preceding note is to be continued above a changing bass (see Ex.5a).

EXAMPLE 5a  5b

In practice, the stroke is often omitted where it is obvious that a chord should not be changed, so that the dash after the $\frac{6}{5}$ on E♭ in Ex.5a is not strictly necessary. When a horizontal dash continues over several beats, it is often a good idea for the upper parts to adapt the distribution of the chord. The first bar of Ex.5a could be rewritten as shown in Ex.5b.

Keyboard writing

The examples given so far have all been for keyboard, and you will notice that the textures are very simple. Most of the chords are in four parts, with three notes played by the right hand; some are in three parts; one is in five parts (Ex.2 last bar); and one is in only two parts (Ex.3, bar 2, 3rd beat). When writing for keyboard you can vary the number of notes in your chords, but care must be given to the way in which the notes are spaced. An interval of an octave or more between the bass note and the next note above it is perfectly acceptable, and can be particularly effective when the bass note is low. Conversely, wide gaps between any of the upper parts should always be avoided. A $\frac{5}{3}$ chord on low G, if laid out as in Ex.6a, lacks cohesion because of the wide interval in the middle of the chord. Ex.6b shows various ways in which the chord could be laid out more effectively.

EXAMPLE 6a  6b

One way of ensuring that there are no untoward gaps in the middle of your chords is to use the left hand exclusively for the bass part, giving all other notes to the right hand and spacing them closely enough together to lie easily under the fingers. Aim for a four-part texture (one note in the left hand, three in the right), reducing to three parts when the bass note is high but you want the rest of the chord to lie in the middle or low register of the treble-clef stave. Chords in more than four parts should be used very rarely; reserve them for points such as cadences where you want a richer sonority.

When laying out $\frac{5}{3}$, $\frac{6}{3}$ and $\frac{6}{4}$ chords in four parts, one note must be doubled at the octave. There is no hard-and-fast rule about which note to double, but here is a useful guide:

$\frac{5}{3}$: double the bass note or the 5.

$\frac{6}{3}$: when the interval between the 6 and 3 is a perfect 4th, double a note other than the bass note; when the interval between the 6 and 3 is an augmented 4th, double the bass note.

$\frac{6}{4}$: double the bass note.

In keyboard realisations of Baroque continuo parts you will sometimes see four-note chords (the $\frac{7}{5}$, $\frac{6}{5}$, $\frac{6}{4}$ and $\frac{6}{4}$) reduced to three parts. When one of the notes is left out, the character of the chord is changed. It is therefore safer to lay out four-note chords in full, with the exception only of the $\frac{7}{5}$ from which the 5 may be omitted without much loss of colour.

Because figured bass uses numerals, beginners sometimes fall into the trap of thinking they can compose by numbers without trying to imagine how the music they are writing will sound. Seeing a $\frac{5}{3}$ chord on C, they immediately double the C at the octave and write the notes E and G above it before moving on to the next bass note, which is realised without thought to how it might relate to the chord they have just written or the chord above the next bass note. Ex.7a shows what can happen when exercises are worked in this way. Each chord, taken in isolation, is laid out correctly, but when the chords are played in succession the music sounds very disconnected. The top part leaps about in a most illogical way, and the passage is full of consecutive perfect 5ths and octaves. The reason why these consecutive perfect consonances should be avoided is that the intervals, being so strong in themselves, reinforce a melodic line and make it stand out too prominently. This is really an aspect of part-writing (see *AB Guide*, Part II, 16/2); but you should bear in mind that, although a predominantly chordal texture is expected in the examination tests, the horizontal element of the music (including the melodic logic of the top and inner parts of the chords) cannot be disregarded.

EXAMPLE 7a

A more effective working is shown in Ex.7b. Notice the shape of the top part: most of the time it is in contrary motion to the bass, and further melodic interest is achieved by the pair of quavers at the end of the first bar which use both the 6 and 5 of the ⁶₅ chord on B. Notice, too, how the dissonant intervals (the diminished 5th in bar 1 and the augmented 4th and minor 7th in bar 4) are treated: in each case the notes creating the clash move up or down by step. Finally, notice the way the texture is varied: chords in the higher register all have four notes, while most of those in the lower register have only three.

EXAMPLE 7b

As in the above example, you should always try to give the top part melodic shape, bearing in mind that it is not necessary to write the notes of chords in the order in which the figures appear. Ex.8a, though a perfectly accurate realisation of the figuring, is dull because the top part is confined to two notes. Compare this working with Ex.8b.

EXAMPLE 8a

EXAMPLE 8b

Where possible, you should also try to introduce rhythmic interest into your realisations. When a bass note is held for more than one beat and no change of harmony is indicated, it is often a good idea for the notes of the chord to be redistributed in the upper parts. Compare Ex.9a, which is rhythmically very dull, with Ex.9b.

EXAMPLE 9a

9b

When realising figured basses for keyboard, do not make the music too elaborate. Close-position chords (i.e. chords in which the upper notes are spaced as closely together as possible) will ensure that the music is not too difficult and will be equally effective on organ or harpsichord (the two keyboard instruments most frequently used for continuo playing during the figured-bass period) or on the modern piano. It is advisable not to make the compass of the right-hand part too wide: generally speaking you should keep to the stave, and in no circumstances go beyond two ledger lines above or below it.

With regard to notating keyboard music, notes of a chord can share a single stem and should do so whenever possible. Only when the parts do not move together is it necessary to combine upward and downward stems. Look back at the examples given so far to see how they are notated; you will learn much by copying them out (but *not* Exs.6a, 7a, 8a or 9a!).

Writing for voices

When realising a figured bass for four-part voices you must of course maintain a four-part texture throughout. This means that when the chord is a triad you must decide which note to double; and the advice given above about laying out $\frac{5}{3}$, $\frac{6}{3}$ and $\frac{6}{4}$ chords in four parts for keyboard holds good for four-part vocal writing, though notes can now be doubled either at the octave or at the unison. It should be emphasised, however, that the vertical sounds (the chords) are only part of the texture, and in four-part writing the melodic logic of the individual parts and the relationship of each part to the others are equally important. Good part-writing, whether for voices or an instrumental ensemble, is essentially a compromise between vertical and horizontal elements.

To see how this works in practice, look at this example of four-part vocal writing.

Chorale: 'Lobe den Herren' (*Stralsund Gesangbuch*, 1665)

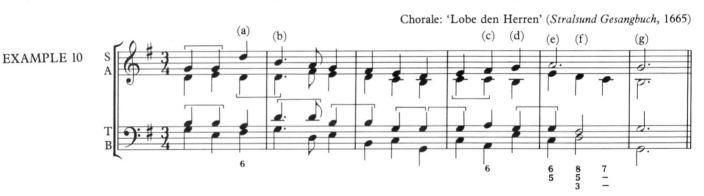

EXAMPLE 10

The first thing to notice is that the soprano is the most tuneful part. The alto and tenor are relatively unadventurous but are not without melodic interest. When realising figured basses for SATB, it is a good idea to sketch in the whole of the soprano part first.
The alto and tenor parts can then be added to complete the harmony; and although they will tend to have more repeated or sustained notes than the top part, you should try to make them as interesting as possible. When you have sketched out your working, sing or play each of the upper voice parts to make sure none of them contains any intervals which are difficult to sing. Major 7ths and all augmented and diminished intervals can come into this category, and although these melodic intervals are used by various composers (e.g. by J. S. Bach in his chorale harmonisations), they are best avoided at this stage. It is a good plan to play the tenor and bass together; then alto, tenor and bass; and finally all four parts. You will not be able to do this in the examination room, of course, but in the early stages it is an excellent way of finding out how the parts work against each other. You should also go through each *pair* of parts to make sure there are no consecutive perfect consonances (unisons, 5ths, octaves). There are six separate pairs to check: S/A, S/T, S/B, A/T, A/B and T/B.

Other points to notice about Ex.10 are:

1) The compass of each voice part is comfortably within its normal range. The approximate ranges of soprano, alto, tenor and bass voices are set out in *AB Guide*, Part II, 14/1, but it must be emphasised that untrained singers may often have a more limited range, particularly at the upper end of the compass. Even trained singers can find it tiring to sing a long line of very high notes. Notes towards the top of the compass should therefore be used sparingly and are easier to sing when approached by a series of small steps rather than by leaps.

2) The spacing between the bass and tenor parts is carefully managed so that the widest interval (here it is an octave) is used whenever the bass is lower than C, and intervals of less than a 5th are not used when the bass is lower than D. This illustrates an important principle: close spacing between bass and tenor parts should be avoided when the bass is in the lower part of its register. In this particular passage the interval between the notes of any two adjacent voice parts (soprano and alto, alto and tenor, tenor and bass) is never more than an octave. You will often find intervals greater than an octave between tenor and bass parts, though not between any other pair of adjacent voices. The comments made on p.6 about spacing of chords for keyboard hold good when writing for four-part voices: wide gaps in the middle of the texture should be avoided but can be very effective at the bottom of chords.

3) Where two adjacent chords have one or more notes in common, these notes (shown by square brackets) are in the same part. This helps to bind the chords together and at the same time ensures smooth part-writing. As a general rule it is a good idea to bind chords together in this way, but there are occasions when it is more important to give one or more of the voice parts an interesting melodic shape. Slavish adherence to the principle of keeping notes common to adjacent chords in the same part can lead to a succession of repeated notes which is dull to sing and can be dull to listen to.

4) Of the twelve $\frac{5}{3}$ chords in the extract, the bass note is doubled in all but two of them. The exceptions are the chords at (b) and (d). In (b), a major triad, the alto and tenor double the 5 at the unison; in (d), a minor triad, the 3 is doubled at the octave.

5) There are two $\frac{6}{3}$ chords. In the chord at (a) the interval between the 6 and 3 is a perfect 4th, so the bass note is not doubled. In the chord at (c) the bass note is the one to be doubled because the interval between the 6 and 3 is an augmented 4th.

6) The chord at (e) is a $\frac{6}{5}$. The 5 in the tenor, which clashes with the 6 in the soprano, is prepared (i.e. sounded) in the previous chord. The dissonance is resolved by the tenor falling a semitone to F♯ in the chord at (f) while the soprano stays on A.

7) The 8 to 7 progression at (f) is treated by giving both notes to the same part – the alto. This is a common melodic progression, but sometimes the dissonant 7th is approached by leap. Where 8 is to move to 7 in the exercises at the end of this section (and in similar ones in the examination papers) it will be shown in the figuring, as it is here (i.e. $\frac{8\ \ 7}{5\ \ -}$).
Where a chord is figured simply as 7 (implying $\frac{7}{5}$), the 7 may be approached by leap or by step; the latter is more usual in vocal music from the figured-bass period.

8) The final chord at (g) is a $\frac{5}{3}$, but the 5 is omitted. This is because the natural movement of the two inner parts – F♯ in the tenor wanting to rise to G, C in the alto needing to fall to B – is not at odds with the desired sonority of the final chord. You will often see cadences in chorales and hymn tunes where the leading note does not rise to the tonic but falls to the 5 of the tonic chord. If it did so here, the final chord would have a much darker colour because the tenor would be only a 5th above the low G in the bass part (see point 2 above). Note, however, that the dissonant 7th in the $\frac{7}{5}$ chord must always be resolved downwards by step.

Bearing in mind the points made about Ex.10, look at the realisation below which can be used as a model for your own workings. You will notice that at the cadence the leading note (given to the alto) does *not* rise to the tonic. On this occasion, a fuller sonority is desirable for the final chord, and this is more important than the melodic shape of one of the inner parts. You will also notice that in the final chord the interval between the tenor and bass is greater than an octave. This brightens the sound and is a good example of how wide spacing at the bottom of a chord can be used to good effect. It should be emphasised, however, that under no circumstances should you have more than an octave between the soprano and alto or between the alto and tenor parts.

EXAMPLE 11

Exercise 1 Writing for four-part voices (SATB) or keyboard, realise the chords indicated. Assume that all chords are $\frac{5}{3}$ unless otherwise shown.

B Harmonising melodies

The chords to be identified in Grade 5 were the tonic, subdominant and dominant, together with the supertonic. A lot can be done with these four chords, and you will find quite lengthy passages in many different kinds of music which use only these chords set out in root position or first inversion. Second-inversion chords are used more rarely except at cadence points, where the $\frac{6}{4} : \frac{5}{3}$ progression on the dominant (Ic–V) is a common formula.

In Grade 6, the harmonic vocabulary is extended to chords derived from triads on any degree of the major or minor scale. The syllabus also introduces chords which include the 7th above the root as well as the 3rd and 5th. The construction of these added 7th chords is described in *AB Guide*, Part I, p.61. It is of course possible to add 7ths to triads on any degree of the scale, but at this stage 7th chords and their inversions are confined to those on the supertonic (root position and first inversion only) and dominant notes (any position). These chords are frequently used at cadence points because of the need for the dominant 7th to be resolved. Just as the progression V7–I is a more compelling form of the perfect cadence than V–I (see *AB Guide*, Part I, 9/2b), so the dominant chord (with or without added 7th) is prepared more powerfully when preceded by the supertonic 7th either in root position (II7) or first inversion (II7b). The imperfect cadence II–V is thus stronger as II7–V, and the supertonic chord with added 7th is often used to precede the dominant 7th at perfect cadences. The progression II7–V7–I is very common at final cadences; even more common is the progression II7b–V7–I.

EXAMPLE 12

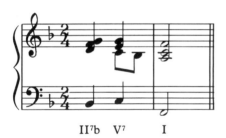

II7b   V7   I

The choice of suitable chords to harmonise melodies at cadential points was a requirement of the Grade 5 syllabus. In Grade 6 you will be asked to harmonise complete melodies, and you will be given the choice of two different exercises. In the first you will be asked to select suitable chords to accompany a short diatonic melody (most melodies will be about eight bars long) in any major or minor key. The chords can be shown by the Roman numeral system or, if you prefer, by letter names as in jazz notation. (These two methods of indicating chords are discussed in more detail below.) The alternative is to provide a bass to a given melody and to indicate the harmonies by providing figures. These exercises are essentially the same: each tests your ability to provide a chordal accompaniment to a given melodic line. The only real difference is in the method of indicating the chords, though the melodies for the first alternative are likely to cover a wider range of styles than those for the second which will be taken from music composed during the figured-bass period.

A melody can be harmonised in various ways. There is no single solution which is correct and, although some harmonisations may be better than others, there will usually be several versions which are equally effective. Some of the melodies in the exercises at the end of this section are taken from works by known composers, as are some you will find in the examination papers. In such cases you are not expected to reproduce the composer's original harmonies. You will get full credit for any harmonisation which works, however different it may be from what the composer actually wrote.

A good harmonisation is one in which the melody is supported by appropriate chords set out so that they move smoothly from one to another. You have already discovered at Grade 5 how chords on the tonic, supertonic, subdominant and dominant can be used at cadence points, and you are familiar with the following cadential progressions:

1) V–I (the perfect cadence);
2) IV–I (the plagal cadence);
3) I–V, II–V and IV–V (imperfect cadences).

It should be emphasised that use of these progressions is not confined to cadences. The progression V–I, for example, can occur at the beginning or in the middle of a phrase, as can the progression I–V. The opening of the Hornpipe from Handel's *Water Music* Suite No.2 is based entirely on tonic and dominant chords:

EXAMPLE 13a

Although only two chords are used in this phrase, the harmony is never dull. This is partly because in the first three bars the pattern of change between tonic and dominant chords is varied (but notice that there is *always* a change from the last beat of one bar to the first beat of the next), and partly because the two notes marked with asterisks in bars 3 and 4 are treated as non-harmony notes.[1] Much of the interest, however, is due to the fact that Handel mixes root-position ($\frac{5}{3}$) chords with chords in first inversion ($\frac{6}{3}$). The mixture of $\frac{5}{3}$ and $\frac{6}{3}$ chords allows more variety of harmonic colour and at the same time makes it possible for the bass part to have a more interesting shape. If we re-harmonise the passage using only root-position chords, a great deal of interest is lost.

EXAMPLE 13b

First inversions are often used instead of root positions, especially when the melody note is the root or 5th of the chord. When the melody note is the 3rd of the triad, it is usually better for the supporting chord to be in root position, though the mediant note can sometimes be harmonised by chord Ib. The leading note, however, should *never* be harmonised by chord Vb, because it will result in consecutive octaves between the melody and bass parts.

EXAMPLE 14

---

[1]Throughout Section B of this book asterisks are used in the music examples to indicate non-harmony notes. The various kinds of non-harmony note are described in *AB Guide*, Part II, 15/1–7.

The primary triads

The tonic and dominant chords are the most important in tonal harmony because of the magnetic pull between them. The next chord in order of importance is the subdominant (chord IV), which is the third of the three primary triads. It can be used as an alternative to chord I to harmonise the tonic note, and it is the only primary triad which can be used to harmonise the 4th and 6th degrees of the diatonic scale.

Use of the three primary triads close together is a very strong way of stating the key at the beginning of a piece (see Ex.15) or at the beginning of a new section when there has been a change of key (see Ex.16).

Composers sometimes write quite lengthy passages using only chords I, IV and V. A good example is the opening of the last movement of Beethoven's Fifth Symphony. The symphony is in C minor, which is the main key of the first and third movements. The fourth and final movement is in C *major*, however, and to emphasise the new key Beethoven bases the first 34 bars of his finale entirely on the three primary triads, set out in root position or first inversion. Ex.17 shows the opening bars of this finale. Some instrumental parts have been left out to make the passage easier to play on the keyboard.

You will notice that in this example non-harmony notes occur in the bass as well as in the melody. This makes the bass part more interesting in bars 8 and 10, where the quaver figure is an inversion of the melody in bars 7 and 9. Passing notes and auxiliary notes can be introduced into bass parts to keep the rhythm going when the melody is still, to make the bass more shapely, and (as here) to imitate fragments of the melody. Generally, however, bass parts have less movement than the melodies above them except in contrapuntal music.

Beethoven's use of chords I, IV and V in this passage makes the harmony very bold and solid. The key of C major is firmly established in the first six bars by the constant to-and-fro of tonic and dominant chords, and the magnetic pull of the tonic is made more compelling by the addition of the 7th to the dominant triads in bars 2 and 3. The introduction of the subdominant chord in bar 7 brings variety to the harmony and at the same time confirms C as the tonal centre. Play through this passage, and if possible listen to a recording of the work, in order to see how chords I, IV and V/V^7 work together to produce a strong sense of key.

A lot of traditional folk and pop music is based on the three primary triads.

EXAMPLE 18

Spiritual: 'When the saints go marching in'

This spiritual has become a standard jazz number. You will often hear it played with more sophisticated harmonies (jazz musicians frequently add extra notes to triads to make the chords more interesting, and even replace simple diatonic chords with more chromatic ones built on a different root), but the harmonic basis of the melody is as shown in Ex.18. Rests have been placed beneath the first three crotchet notes because it is not appropriate for this anacrusis to be harmonised.

Deciding when to change chords

You will notice that in Ex.18 there are very few chord changes until the last three bars. The speed of this melody is quick, and if we were to harmonise every note the music would sound very cluttered. By contrast, every note but one of the hymn tune in Ex.15 is harmonised with a different chord. Most hymn tunes are harmonised in this way, with a change of chord on each of the main beats of the bar.

Changing to a new chord or to a different position of the same chord has the effect of stressing the melody note because it introduces a new harmonic colour. When a composer wishes to emphasise every note of his melody, he harmonises each note with a different chord. This is often done to make the music sound solemn (as in Ex.16) or majestic (as in Ex.13a). There are passages in many different kinds of music, vocal and instrumental, in which there is a change of chord for every note, or almost every note, of the melody. Here are some more examples, though in these the harmony is not confined to the primary triads:

EXAMPLE 19a

Handel: 'Worthy is the Lamb' from *Messiah*
(voice parts and basso continuo only)

EXAMPLE 19b

EXAMPLE 19c

In each of these passages the harmonic rhythm (i.e. the rhythmic pattern produced by chord changes) is identical to the rhythm of the melodic line, except for the appoggiatura at the end of the Wagner example. However, not all melodies can be harmonised successfully in this way. If we try to harmonise the tune 'Lavender's blue' with a different chord for every note, it will sound very awkward.

EXAMPLE 20a

I Vb V I V⁷b I V I   IV IVc IVb IV   I Vb V I V⁷b I V I   IV Ic V⁷ I

The principal reason why this harmonisation does not work is that rhythmically unimportant notes are given as much stress as those falling on the strong first beat of the bar. This destroys the simple, lilting rhythm of the melody. What is needed here is a change of chord only where the main accents fall, that is on the first beat of each bar. There is, of course, a subsidiary accent on the fourth quaver beat but, as no change of harmony is suggested by the melody, it is better to keep to one chord in each of the first three bars. Notice, though, that the working shown in Ex.20b uses four chords in the final bar, one for each melody note. This quickening of the harmonic rhythm makes the cadence more emphatic. Composers often increase the rate of harmonic change when approaching final cadences.

EXAMPLE 20b

I   IV   I   IV Ic V⁷ I

These two harmonisations of 'Lavender's blue' illustrate how important it is for the harmonic rhythm to be in keeping with the style of the melody. Slow-moving melodies need more chord changes to keep them going, and very long notes may need to be supported by more than one chord. Melodies in which there are a lot of quick notes need fewer chord changes, as do those in a simple flowing style.

Here is another melody in $\frac{6}{8}$ time. It moves at about the same speed as 'Lavender's blue' ($\bullet. = c.50$), but in this case a change of chord on the second dotted crotchet beat is a good idea because the melody notes in the second half of the bar suggest chord V^7, not chord I. Furthermore, there are no busy semiquaver groups in this melody, so two chords per bar will help to keep the rhythm going.

American folk-song: 'The streets of Laredo'

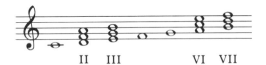

Tempo indications and dynamic markings, if there are any, can often provide useful clues to the style of a melody and help you to decide how often to change chords. After that, you need to decide which notes should be treated as harmony notes and which should not. This is quite difficult for beginners; so to help you in the early stages, asterisks are placed above all non-harmony notes in the first ten melodies in Exercise 2 on pp.26–27.

Secondary triads

The secondary triads are built on the 2nd, 3rd, 6th and 7th degrees of the scale. In the key of C major their roots are D, E, A and B:

These chords are of two types: three of them (II, III and VI) are minor chords; chord VII is diminished. By combining secondary triads with the primary triads, all of which are major chords, we add greatly to the variety of harmonic colour available.

A good way of exploring the harmonic function of the secondary triads is to consider their relationship to the primary chords. For example, chord II can in certain contexts be used as an alternative to chord IV. The cadential progression II–V–I is very similar in effect to the progression IV–V–I, as you have already discovered in your work for Grade 5. This is because chords II and IV have two notes in common:

If we add a 7th to chord II the relationship is even closer:

Similarly, chords VII and V^7 are closely related:

Chord III has two notes in common with the primary triads whose roots lie a 3rd either side of it:

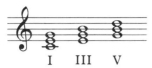

EXAMPLE 26

It can sometimes be used instead of chord I to harmonise the mediant or dominant note, and in some contexts offers an alternative to chord V for the dominant or leading note.

Likewise, chord VI is related to chords IV and I:

EXAMPLE 27

It is occasionally used in place of chord IV (compare the progressions I–IV–V with I–VI–V, and I–IV–II–V with I–VI–II–V), and is often used to interrupt an expected perfect cadence (see *AB Guide*, Part I, 9/2e). It should be emphasised, however, that the secondary triads are not interchangeable with the primary triads. Each chord has its own individual colour and harmonic function which you must learn to feel and then use for its own sake.

The secondary triads are particularly useful when harmonising melodies which incorporate stepwise movement. To illustrate this, let us look at two possible ways of harmonising a short hymn-tune-like phrase with a different chord for each note. The first uses only primary triads, though a 7th is added to chord V at the cadence.

EXAMPLE 28

There is nothing really wrong with this harmonisation, though the progression V–IV in bar 1 is a little awkward. Consecutive root-position chords on notes a tone or semitone apart are best avoided when the bass is in parallel motion with the melody, because the ear hears consecutive parallel 5ths even when, as here, they are not actually present in the part-writing. The reason for this is that the perfect 12th (a compound perfect 5th) is one of the most prominent notes in the harmonic series. When the bass and melody move in consecutive 10ths, the resulting parallel 5ths in the overtones are clearly audible. Consecutive 5ths can be heard again in bar 2, where we have used the progression IV–V. This is a standard progression in music of all kinds (it is often used to form an imperfect cadence or to precede chord I at final cadences), but for the reason just given the progression works best when the melody and bass are in contrary motion:

EXAMPLE 29

The problem of implied consecutive 5ths can be avoided if we substitute secondary triads for some of the primary chords. The combination of primary and secondary triads will also enable us to make the harmony more varied and to give the bass part a more interesting shape.

EXAMPLE 30

This harmonisation uses all four of the secondary triads (as does the chorale harmonisation shown in Ex. 10 of Section A). Notice in particular the progression I–V–VI–III at the beginning. This progression is often used to harmonise descending scales and is very effective because of the sequential pattern of the bass. You should memorise this progression and also the progression IV–VIIb–I (bar 2), trying them in different keys. If you experiment with chord VII, you will find it sounds best in first inversion: diminished triads are used most frequently in this position. The cadential progression II⁷b–V–I should also be memorised. It is one of the most effective and frequently used progressions at final cadences.

The secondary triads used in conjunction with primary triads also make it possible to write more interesting and varied harmony in pieces where it is not appropriate to have a different chord for every note of the melody. The sea shanty 'Spanish ladies' is in $\frac{3}{4}$ time, but the tempo is fairly quick and there is a strong feeling of one dotted minim beat in each bar, not three crotchets. The first phrase of the melody suggests movement between tonic and dominant chords but, if we try to harmonise it with these chords only, we cannot make chord changes where we need to. Chord I must be used throughout the first two bars, and V for the next two.

EXAMPLE 31a

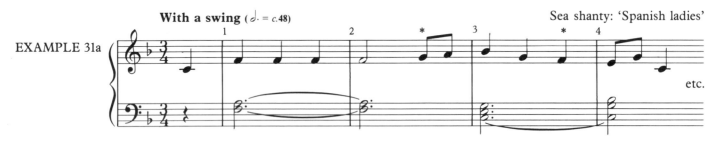

This is not very effective because the harmonic rhythm does not match the rhythm of the melody. Sing the tune, observing the given style indication and tempo marking, and you will find you are making a natural stress on the first beat of each bar. What is needed, therefore, is a change of chord after each bar-line to emphasise the swinging rhythm. It is possible to do this by introducing two of the secondary triads.

EXAMPLE 31b

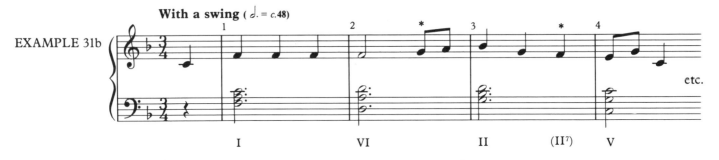

The progression I–VI–II–V is another you should memorise and try out in various keys. It is particularly effective because of the strong root movement: down a 3rd, up a 4th, down a 5th.

Harmony in minor keys

The melodies we have harmonised so far have all been in major keys, and the chords used have all been derived from the notes of the diatonic major scale. Chords used to harmonise melodies in minor keys are derived from the minor scale.

When the minor scale appears in its harmonic form, it produces the following primary triads:

EXAMPLE 32
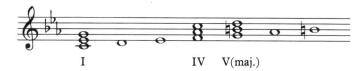

Notice that chords I and IV are minor, but chord V is *major*. It is important to remember to include the raised leading note (B♮ in the key of C minor) when writing perfect and imperfect cadences:

EXAMPLE 33
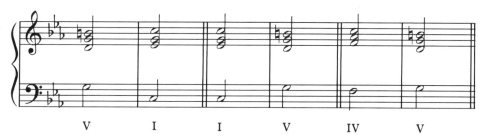

These cadences are just as strong in the minor key as they are in the major.

The harmonic minor scale produces the following secondary triads:

EXAMPLE 34
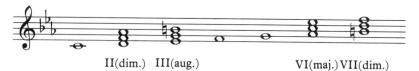

As you can see, one of these (chord VI) is a major triad, two are diminished (II and VII), and one is augmented (III). Chords II, VI and VII have the same harmonic function in the minor key as in the major, and can be used in similar contexts. Chord III needs special handling, however, because of the augmented 5th. This chord is rarely used in minor harmony, and will not be needed for harmonising any melody set in the Grade 6 examination.

It is the harmonic form of the minor scale which provides the basis for harmony in minor keys:

Chorale: 'Herzliebster Jesu'

EXAMPLE 35

There are numerous different harmonisations of this chorale melody, some of them quite elaborate. Here we have used only primary triads, and you will notice that they work together in precisely the same way as they do in major keys. Indeed, most of what has been said about chord relationships in the major key holds good for the minor.

When a minor melody uses only notes found in the harmonic minor scale, it can be harmonised with chords from those shown in Ex.32 together with all but one of the chords in Ex. 34. More often than not, however, melodies depart from the harmonic minor scale to avoid the awkward interval between the submediant note (A♭ in the key of C minor) and the leading note (B♮) an augmented 2nd above it. When a melody moves by step between or through these notes, the 6th degree of the scale is raised on the way up (see Ex.36a) and the 7th degree is lowered on the way down (see Ex.36b):

You will recognise these patterns as belonging to the *melodic* minor scale.

If we build triads on each note of the ascending melodic minor scale, we find that four of them (I, III, V and VII) are the same as the corresponding triads in the harmonic minor. Three of them are different, however. Chord II has a raised 5th (converting it from a diminished to a minor triad); chord IV has a raised 3rd and becomes a major triad; and chord VI has a raised root, making it a diminished triad. Here is the scale with all its triads; the three chords that cannot be formed from the harmonic minor scale are marked with a cross.

 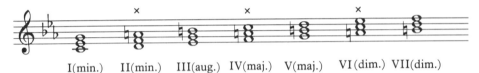

In its descending form the melodic minor scale produces three other chords which cannot be made out of the harmonic minor. One of these (chord V) is minor; the other two (VII and III) are major. Unlike chord III (aug.), chord III (maj.) is often used in minor harmony.

 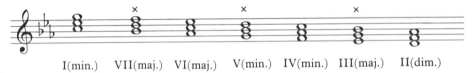

The tonic chord is the only one which is the same in both forms of the melodic minor scale. Every other chord is variable, but it is seldom difficult to decide which form to use because the harmony must always match the movement of the melody. A melodic figure ascending from the dominant to the tonic could be harmonised as in Ex.38a or Ex.38b:

 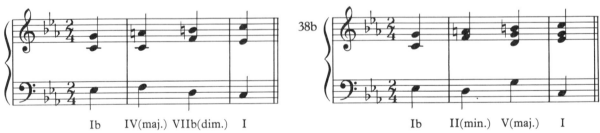

while a figure descending by step from the tonic might be harmonised as in Ex.39a or Ex.39b:

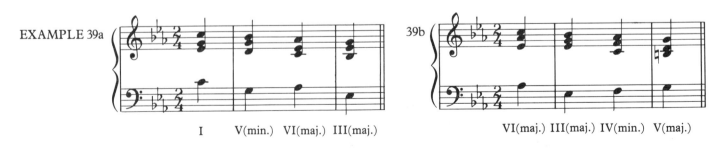

Sometimes, chords from the melodic minor scale are used when they are not strictly required by the notes of the melody. The refrain of this well-known carol does not rise above the subdominant note or go below the leading note, so it is quite possible to harmonise it diatonically (i.e. with chords derived from the harmonic minor scale):

Coventry Carol

The melody ends with a *tierce de Picardie* (see *AB Guide*, Part II, p.147), but apart from this final chord the harmony is rather dull. We could make it more varied and interesting by introducing chords from the melodic minor (descending form) in bars 3 and 5. Notice the downward stepwise movement of the bass part in bars 2–4. This pattern is often used in minor harmony.

Chord symbols

In all but one of the music examples given so far the harmony has been written out in full to make it clear how the various chords are constructed. Roman numerals have usually been added beneath the chords to help you to see what they are and how they relate to each other. In the examination you are not asked to plan or notate the complete texture but simply to indicate suitable chords using either Roman numerals or letter names.

The Roman numeral system is outlined in *AB Guide*, Part I, 8/1–2 and discussed more fully in *AB Guide*, Part II, Appendix D. The basic system is perfectly adequate for describing diatonic chords in the major key, but difficulties arise in the minor key, where every chord except the tonic is variable (and the tonic chord itself may be altered from minor to major at final cadences). When harmonising melodies in minor keys, it is *essential* to show for each chord whether you intend it to be major, minor or diminished. If you use 'Basic Roman' (the system outlined in the above-mentioned Appendix), you can do this by adding **maj., min.** or **dim.** in brackets after the Roman numeral – e.g. II(min.), VI(maj.) – or to save space, beneath the numeral – e.g. $\underset{\text{(min.)}}{\text{II}}$. If you do not do this, it will be assumed that each chord is to be formed from the notes of the harmonic minor scale.

Some people use a combination of Roman numerals and figured-bass notation – a system sometimes called 'Figured Roman'. This is described in *AB Guide*, Part II, Appendix D. Like Basic Roman, Figured Roman does not indicate whether chords are major, minor or diminished, so that, if you use this system, you will have to add the relevant information – e.g. V_3^6(min.), II_5^6(dim.).

A third method of indicating chords by Roman numerals has been developed from the basic system. This method, called 'Extended Roman' in *AB Guide*, is also described in the same Appendix. It is much less cumbersome than either of the other methods, because it uses the symbol ° to indicate a diminished triad and distinguishes between major and minor chords in a very simple way: upper case, or capital, Roman numerals (e.g. IV, V) are reserved for chords with a major 3rd above the root; lower case, or small, Roman numerals (e.g. iv, v) are used to show that the chord is to have a minor 3rd. This saves you the trouble of writing '(maj.)', '(min.)' or '(dim.)' after the numeral and takes up less space.

When using Extended Roman it is important to make it clear at all times whether upper-case or lower-case numerals are intended. Be careful to add a dot over every 'i' when writing lower-case numerals (e.g. ii, iv); upper-case numerals should be written with horizontal lines (e.g. Ⅲ, Ⅵ) not merely III, VI, as they appear when printed.

Because of its ability to describe more complex chords briefly but precisely, Extended Roman is greatly preferable to the basic system or Figured Roman. When chromatic chords are introduced in Grades 7 and 8, you will find Basic Roman and Figured Roman inadequate, so it is a good idea to start using Extended Roman at this stage, applying it to the major key as well as the minor for the sake of consistency. However, Extended Roman is not a requirement of the Grade 6 syllabus. Any method of indicating chords is acceptable, provided that your intentions are clear.

The chord-notation system based on letter names may be used instead of Roman numerals. This system is outlined in *AB Guide*, Part I, 8/3. Letter-name chord indications (as used in jazz and other forms of pop music) show whether chords are major, minor or diminished as a routine part of the system. However, it is by no means routine practice to show which note should appear in the bass. In jazz, that decision is usually left to the performers, though on rare occasions a bass note may be specified. The importance of choosing the most appropriate position (root, first inversion etc.) for each chord need not be stressed further here; a great deal has already been said about this aspect of harmonising melodies. If you use the letter-name system in the examination, you must always state the bass note for any chord you intend not to be in root position. This can be done by drawing an oblique stroke (/) immediately after the chord description and then writing the letter name of the bass note, e.g. Dm^7/F, meaning:

 EXAMPLE 41a

Alternatively, this chord could be written as Dm^7(bass F). The former method is more convenient because it takes up less space, but note that oblique strokes are often used in jazz and light music with an entirely different meaning – that of indicating the same harmony for the next beat or beats, e.g. $\frac{4}{4}$ F / / C^7 |, another way of writing $\frac{4}{4}$ F F F C^7|.

Where oblique strokes are used to show that a chord is to be repeated, they are written as thick lines and are spaced out according to where the beats fall. Ex.41b illustrates both uses of the oblique stroke:

EXAMPLE 41b

To illustrate the differences between these four notational systems, here are two harmonisations of the same melody, with chord symbols as they would appear in Extended Roman (ER), Basic Roman (BR), Figured Roman (FR) and jazz chord notation (JCN).

EXAMPLE 42a

EXAMPLE 42b

Exercise 2   Using *either* Roman numerals *or* letter names, indicate suitable chords to accompany the melodies on the next three pages. Write the chord symbols under the stave. Show whether chords are major, minor or diminished and indicate the bass note for all chords not in root position. Notes marked with an asterisk in Exercises (a) to (j) should be treated as non-harmony notes (as, of course, should all decorative notes in small print, which are not asterisked). In the examination tests you yourself will have to decide which notes to treat as non-harmony notes; so from Exercise (k) onwards the melodies appear as they will in the examination papers. Melodies which begin with an anacrusis will usually not need a chord until the beginning of the first complete bar.

Exercise 2

Melody and figured bass

The examination paper will always give an alternative melody for harmonisation, asking you to provide a bass part and then add figures to indicate your intended harmonies. If you have worked through the exercises in Section A, you should have no difficulty in using figured-bass notation. The melodies will be taken from Baroque sonatas for a solo instrument and basso continuo, and the passages chosen will be ones in which the bass moves very simply, usually marking a change of chord on each beat of the bar, though more frequent chord changes may occasionally be introduced. The following passage from the second movement of Bach's Sonata in E minor for flute and continuo, BWV 1034, is a typical example.

EXAMPLE 43

In the examination tests, the first few notes of the bass part will be given. Here it might be the whole of the first bar and the first note of the second. Cover up the bass part from this point onwards and consider how you might continue it. Does the rest of the flute part imply a change of chord on each crotchet beat? It certainly does in bars 2 and 3, because the rhythm in these two bars is exactly the same as the rhythm in bar 1. There is therefore no reason to change the rhythm of the bass, so you should go on, as Bach does, with the pattern established in bar 1. Look more closely at the flute part, and you will see that the melodic shape of bar 2 is virtually the same as bar 1 (the only difference is the interval between the last two quavers), and that the figure is repeated again in bar 3. This makes a melodic sequence, each bar starting a 3rd lower than the previous one, so the bass part should also move sequentially. The sequence is broken in bar 4, so now the pattern of the bass part must also be changed. Look ahead, and you will see that the music is approaching a perfect cadence, even though the flute part continues the semiquaver figure. (In the examination tests, solo parts will sometimes be adapted to make a cadence more obvious.) To make this cadence more emphatic, it would be a good idea to increase the rate of harmonic change before the $^{6}_{4}{:}^{5}_{\sharp}$ progression, and this is precisely what Bach does. Notice that the second B in this bar is figured $^{5}_{\sharp}$, not $^{5}_{3}$. In minor keys, the dominant chord must always have a raised 3 when it is followed by the tonic chord to form a perfect cadence.

The clues to this harmonisation are nearly all contained in the first bar. The first two notes of the bass part establish the harmonic rhythm, and $^{6}_{3}$ chords on the third and fourth beats suggest how to deal with the corresponding beats of bars 2 and 3. All that is left to do is identify the cadence and then consider how to approach it.

Before working through Exercise 3, look at the extract on the next page from a solo sonata by Handel. It is the beginning of another Allegro movement, this one in a major key.

EXAMPLE 44

As in the Bach example, the harmonic rhythm is established in the first bar, the bass part moving in dotted crotchets. Notice, though, that quaver movement is introduced in the second half of bar 2 to keep the rhythm going when the solo part is rested. The only other place where the bass does not move in dotted crotchets is in bar 6: this is another instance of the rate of harmonic change being accelerated as a cadence is approached.

Here are some other points to notice about this extract:

1) The bass part moves mainly by step. This makes a smooth counter-melody to the solo part, with its frequent leaps.

2) The two high Gs in the solo part in bar 1 are really unaccented passing notes, transposed (together with the Fs that follow them) an octave higher.

3) The first half of bar 3 (with the upbeat at the end of bar 2) is repeated an octave lower in the second half of the bar. The two figures are harmonised in identical fashion.

4) During the 1st and 3rd crotchet beats of bar 5, the solo part plays all the notes of the accompanying chord. When harmonising melodies, look at *groups* of notes to see if they imply a particular chord. Arpeggio figures will often suggest which chord to use, as they do here.

5) There is a V–VI progression in the middle of bar 5. Consecutive $\frac{5}{3}$ chords on notes a tone apart are normally avoided, except when the bass moves up from the dominant note to the submediant in contrary motion to the melody. Conversely, consecutive $\frac{6}{3}$ chords on notes a tone or a semitone apart are frequently used and are always effective. They occur here in bars 1 and 2.

6) At the end of bar 5, Handel is careful to write a $\frac{6}{3}$ chord on the leading note rather than a $\frac{5}{3}$ chord on F, so avoiding a V–I progression so soon before the final cadence. In your own workings, always look for ways of keeping the harmony going so that you do not anticipate perfect cadences with root-position V–I chord progressions.

Exercise 3 Complete the bass parts in the passages on the next four pages. Indicate suitable harmonies by providing figures. End each exercise with a perfect cadence in the tonic key unless otherwise instructed. In Exercises (a) to (d), notes which should be treated as non-harmony notes are marked with asterisks.

Exercise 3

(a) VIOLIN — Allegro — Corelli

(b) FLUTE — Presto — C. P. E. Bach (adapted)

End with an imperfect cadence

(c) FLUTE — Allegro — Handel

FLUTE
[Tempo di Minuetto]   J. S. Bach

(d)

End in the relative major

OBOE   **Larghetto**   Handel

(e)

VIOLIN **Allegro**   Telemann

(f)

VIOLIN **[Tempo di Minuetto]**   Handel

(g)

End in the relative major

VIOLIN [Allegro] Sir Francis Bacon's Masque I (adapted)

(h)

6♯

FLUTE Lentement Loeillet

(i)

6   ♮   6

VIOLIN Vivace Telemann

(j)

6   6
      5

End with an imperfect cadence

C Melodic composition

In the Grade 6 examination you will be asked to compose a melody for a specified instrument, using a given opening. You will be able to choose between extending an opening that implies melodic writing of the kind to be found in music from the 18th and 19th centuries, and extending a specially written opening in a more modern style.

Each given opening will specify the instrument to be used and will have been chosen to take account of the characteristics of that instrument. Although the length of the melody is not specified in the syllabus, it will be made clear in each question in the examination (as it is in the exercises on pp.48–51) what overall length is expected. The most usual request will be for a melody 'of about 16 bars' (which of course includes the given opening) but other possibilities exist, such as 'between 12 and 16 bars', 'between 16 and 20 bars', and so on. The chief reason for this flexibility is that there are so many different ways of developing a given opening successfully that to require a 'regular' 16-bar melody would be unnecessarily restricting, and in any case composers by no means always write in paragraphs of exactly 16 bars. You should aim to achieve the length suggested but it is unlikely that you would be penalised (on grounds of length alone) if your melody reaches a satisfactory conclusion within a bar or two of that length.

You will find a detailed discussion of all aspects of pre-20th-century melodic composition in *The AB Guide to Music Theory*, Part II, Chapter 18, to which constant reference should be made. In addition, *Music Theory in Practice*, Grade 5 (Section I), contains much practical advice on melody writing, together with examples based on 8-bar designs. Since the requirement for Grade 6 in respect of tonal melodic composition is largely an extension of Grade 5 work, the first section below concentrates on outlining the points to be borne in mind when writing longer melodies. The second section discusses various aspects of 'free' melodic composition – that is, composition which is not necessarily bound by the conventions of the tonal period but may instead reflect approaches developed by composers during the 20th century.

Tonal melodic composition

The topics receiving special attention in *AB Guide*, Part II, Chapter 18, include regular and irregular phrasing, antecedent and consequent, melodic sequence, melodic design, use of motifs, phrase overlap, interpolation, cadencing etc. Many examples of melodies from the 18th and 19th centuries are given, some of them in their fully harmonised form. You should *play* the examples in this chapter (or arrange to have them played to you) in order to help develop your aural memory and to give you practice at gauging the overall effect of the longer examples.

It is also essential that you develop your ability to 'hear' what you write, so that when you are in the examination room (where you will not have access to any instrument) you can be confident that your melodic composition will sound as you intend it to sound. You should therefore play your melodies through if you can, either on the piano or, if necessary, on a substitute instrument (e.g. using the violin to play a flute melody). The best training of all would be to hear your melodies played by the 'specified' instruments, though this could well place rather heavy demands on your friends' willingness and abilities! In this way you will gradually acquire some insight into the characteristics of each instrument, and you will start to develop the ability to write idiomatically, i.e. in a style suited to the instrument. The examples on pp.36–47 are taken from a wide range of instrumental and vocal music; in each case, an appropriate 'melody' instrument has been suggested.[1]

You will be expected to add all the necessary performance directions to your completed melody, including appropriate phrase marks and marks of articulation, so that you give a full picture of how you wish it to sound. One difference at Grade 6 is that, normally, performance directions (especially tempo and dynamic level) will be shown for the given opening, even if the original material (e.g. from a Baroque work) had no such markings. Where the material is taken from a musical work and is not written especially for the purposes of this question, the composer's name will usually be given. This is simply to provide an indication of the style or character of the material. For example, if you are extending the opening shown as Exercise 4c on p.48, you should not worry that your melody will be assessed only in relation to what Vivaldi actually wrote; but you should take care that you do not include details that are wildly inconsistent with the style of the period.[2]

The three main categories of tonal melodic composition for the Grade 6 examination are:

1) a melody in the style of the principal melodic part of a Baroque dance movement (such as a Gavotte, Bourrée, Minuet, Sarabande or Gigue) or other movement of simple formal outlines;

2) a balanced Classical melody probably modulating at about the mid-point before returning to the tonic;

3) a melody of a freer design where the opening material develops naturally, modulating to one or more closely related keys before returning to the tonic.

Examples 45 to 54d below fall into the first of these categories. Here is the opening 12-bar sentence of a Bourrée movement written by Handel:

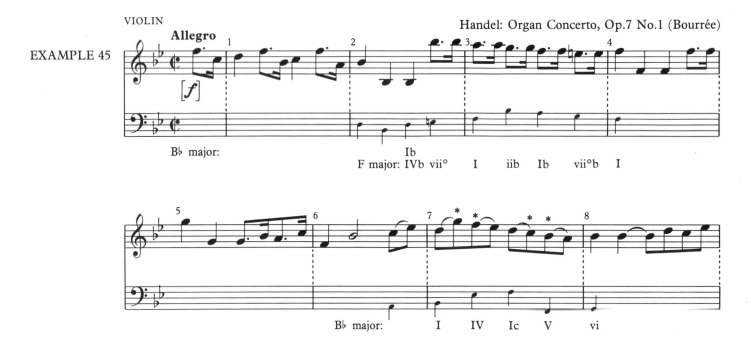

[1]Consult *AB Guide*, Part II, Chapter 22, for more information on instrumental writing. There are many good books on the subject and at this stage you could not do better than to read Gordon Jacob's *Orchestral Technique* (Oxford University Press, available as a paperback). You should try to listen to as much music as you can *while following the printed score*. It does not matter whether the music is 'live' or recorded, as long as you appreciate that reading about instrumental writing is not enough on its own. Your reading must be followed up by experiencing the sounds the instruments make.

[2]A useful book on the features of melodic writing at different periods is Imogen Holst's *Tune* (Faber & Faber, 1962).

You will see that the rhythmic and pitch organisation is already more varied than in the shorter melodies that are quoted in *Music Theory in Practice*, Grade 5. The ♩. ♪ rhythm vanishes after bar 5 in favour of development of two other features – the vigorous note repetition (with or without an octave leap) in bar 2, and the descending scale-fragment from bar 2, 4th beat to the end of bar 3. These contrasting motifs (see *AB Guide*, Part II, 18/7) can be traced easily, though their extension and growth cannot be 'predicted' from the way the melody starts. You will notice that there is a brief modulation into the dominant in bar 4, at what would have been the halfway point for a 'regular' 8-bar sentence. If you play the melody through, omitting bars 7–10, you will see how Handel has extended the second phrase. Handel's bass line and harmonies have been sketched in at the three important cadence-points, using Extended Roman numeral notation (see *AB Guide*, Part II, Appendix D). This method shows both how the modulation is effected in bar 2 and how the melody is decorated with non-harmony notes, which are marked with asterisks. For detailed explanation of modulations, 'pivot' chords etc. see *AB Guide*, Part II, 16/6. You will need to study this Section very carefully.

Examples 48, 50, 53a, 57, 60 and 63 have also been supplied with some indications of the harmony (though not always exactly what the composer wrote) for the reasons just given, and to show how the melodic lines imply certain chord progressions at cadences. You should try to add simple harmonies to the examples below, particularly at the cadence-points. This should help ensure that your own melodies have a reliable harmonic basis. There are very few melodies, of course, which use only harmony notes. Passing notes, upper and lower auxiliary notes, appoggiaturas and other notes of decoration (see *AB Guide*, Part II, 15/1–5) help to make a melody flow and you should aim to include such notes in your own compositions, wherever appropriate. Non-harmony notes have been marked with asterisks in some of the other examples, as follows:

Example 46 – all non-harmony notes;

Examples 49 and 56 – auxiliary notes *only*;

Examples 55 and 61 – appoggiaturas *only*.

Most dance movements from the Baroque period are in **binary form**, a term used to describe a simple structure in two sections, the first usually modulating to another key, the second returning to the original key. Both sections are normally repeated; the musical material of the second section, which is often somewhat longer than the first, is always derived or developed from the material heard earlier. In many movements, even where apparently contrasting material is introduced, the cadence-points are usually found to have similar rhythmic or melodic features. Essentially, binary form is a unified structure in which the second section forms the logical and necessary completion of the first.[1]

---

[1]Binary form is thus distinct from **ternary form**, which describes a musical structure in *three* parts. In ternary movements, the first part ends in the tonic key and the second part, which uses contrasting material, moves straight into a contrasting key; the third part is usually a repeat of the first. One of the clearest examples of this commonly used form is the Minuet and Trio.

The next example shows the first section of another Bourrée, this time by Telemann. Like Ex.45 it lasts for 12 bars; but as it is designed to be the first section of a binary movement, a modulation to the dominant is begun in bar 5, reinforced by sequence and repetition, and brought to a firm cadence in that key in bar 12. In this example, all non-harmony notes have been marked with asterisks.

EXAMPLE 46

VIOLIN

Telemann: *A Musico-Choreographic Wedding Divertissement* (Bourrée)

Another binary movement by Telemann begins as follows:

EXAMPLE 47

FLUTE **Vivace**

Telemann: Fantasie No.9 for unaccompanied flute (4th mvt)

The modulation to the dominant again begins soon after the end of the first 4-bar phrase. Such modulations are often done by introducing the sharpened fourth degree of the scale into the melodic line (i.e. the A♯ in bar 6). This chromatically altered note is of course the leading note of the dominant key and would normally be harmonised by the dominant *chord* of the new key. To introduce the new leading note in this way helps to suggest the new key, which will not be properly established until the perfect cadence at the end of the phrase (a process also to be seen in Ex.46 and in the first section of Ex.52). In Ex.47 you will see that the 16-bar section is really made up from phrases of 4 + 6 + 6 bars, and that the last 6-bar phrase establishes the new key.

The next example, which is the first section of a Minuet, shows a 'regular' construction, with much repetition of the opening two bars. The modulation to the relative major is the most usual one for Baroque movements in a minor key. The sketched-in bass line and harmonies show how Bach reaches the mid-point with an imperfect cadence, starting the modulating process at the end of bar 13. Note how the harmonies are implied by the broken chord shapes of the melodic line.

The Minuet by Handel, Ex.49, is a complete binary movement, with the familiar move to the dominant beginning in bar 6. Notice the importance of the *rhythm* of bar 3, both at the cadences at the end of each section and during the second section where bars 13–16 amount to an 'interpolation' between the antecedent phrase (bars 9–12) and its consequent (bars 17–20). The inversion of the motif marked with a bracket (bars 5–6) should be easy to locate in the second section. As mentioned above, only the auxiliary notes have been marked with asterisks.

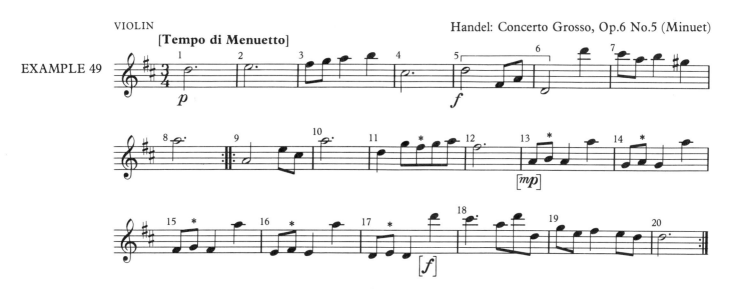

Ex.50 on the next page shows the complete March from *Scipione* by Handel, of which the first 8 bars were quoted in *Music Theory in Practice*, Grade 5 (p.35). The key scheme is a little unusual for a binary movement in that the first section ends in the tonic key rather than in the dominant, which is not used until roughly halfway through the second section. Notice the regularity of the cadencing (alternately imperfect and perfect) which helps give the music the solidity and strength appropriate to a march. The melodic line develops the ascending and descending scale-fragments found in bars 2–4 in a variety of rhythms.

OBOE

Handel: *Scipione* (March)

EXAMPLE 50

Exs.51 & 52 are complete Gavottes by Handel and J.S. Bach. Both composers show great ingenuity in the use of motifs (which are subjected to inversion, sequence and rhythmic displacement) to propel the melodic line forwards while not adding any contrasting material. Variety is also partly achieved by the key schemes, which in each case include a short passage in a minor key just after the double bar. The unity of effect is strengthened in each melody by the rhythmic and motivic repetitions, by the careful preparation for a 'strong' cadence in the tonic at the end, and by the overall shape and balance of the phrases that make up the complete melody. Both melodies demonstrate clearly how the cadences that occur at section ends can have close similarities of rhythm and pitch without being exact repetitions.

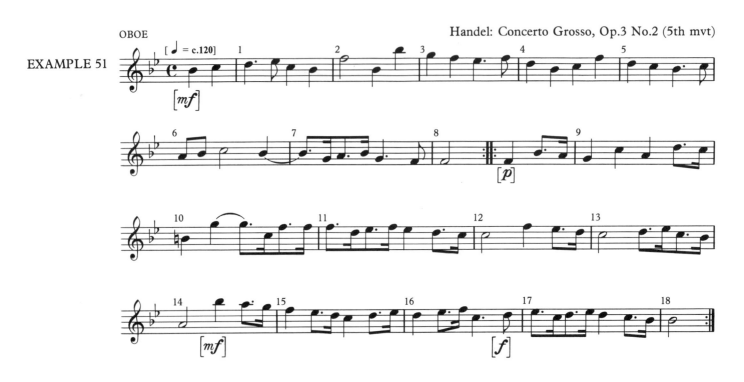

OBOE

Handel: Concerto Grosso, Op.3 No.2 (5th mvt)

EXAMPLE 51

VIOLIN

[Tempo di Gavotta]

J.S. Bach: Suite No.3 in D (3rd mvt)

EXAMPLE 52

In Baroque dance movements it is very unusual for a melody in a major key to modulate either to the subdominant or to the relative minor as its *first* modulation. These keys, particularly the subdominant, will tend to appear as brief modulations in the second sections as, for example, in bars 22–23 in Ex.52. In a minor key movement, a first modulation to the subdominant would be equally unusual, the preferred modulation being either to the relative major (see Ex.48) or to the dominant. The same principles can be found in other 18th-century movements which are not in binary form, as the following extracts from a sonata movement in A minor will show.

FLUTE

Allegro

C. P. E. Bach: Sonata in A minor for flute solo (2nd mvt)

EXAMPLE 53a

A minor: i
C major: vi   iib   V   I

This is how the movement starts; after much contrasting material, the melody returns for a final statement and is varied as shown on the next page:

EXAMPLE 53b
continuing Ex. 53a
from bar 6

Before leaving this section on Baroque melodies, here are some suggestions as to how a given opening, in this case from an Aria by Bononcini (see Ex.54a), might be continued. The examination question for this sort of opening might well be: 'Continue for a further 14 bars or so to make a complete movement in binary form. Modulate to the dominant at the end of the first section.'

EXAMPLE 54a

The two bars given include the following features:
(a) an ascending leap of a 4th, placing the higher note on the 2nd beat of the bar;
(b) two descending leaps outlining a chord (tonic triad);
(c) stepwise movement in bar 2, decorated by a changing note (see *AB Guide*, Part II, 15/4) on the 2nd beat and easily identified by its rhythm (♩ ♫♩).

Clearly these are the features to develop, bearing in mind that it will be characteristic of the period either to make a fairly early move into the dominant or to reach an imperfect cadence at the end of the first phrase (i.e. probably by bar 4). The process of modulation will be assisted if the fourth degree of the home key (the note B♭) is raised to become the leading note (B♮) of the dominant key. The overall suggested length of 16 bars makes it quite likely that regular 2- or 4-bar units will make up an 8 + 8 complete melody. Sequence, phrase repetition, inversion, use of non-harmony notes and, possibly, rhythmic displacement can all be used if they seem appropriate, and as long as they do not detract from a firm cadence at the end of each section. Here is a completed version, composed with due consideration for the above-mentioned points:

EXAMPLE 54b

Ex. 54b clearly has some very serious defects:

1) the inversion of (b) in bar 3 makes a very weak approach to the unconvincing imperfect cadence in bar 4;

2) although the introduction of the B♮ in bar 5 steers the music towards the dominant key, the shape of the second phrase is poor, particularly the leaps in bars 6–7 and the pitches in bars 7 and 8 (with their harmonic implications) which are very weak indeed;

3) the attempted use of sequence in the first half of the second section is very poor, both harmonically and in choice of pitches (for example, the repetition of the note C at the end of bar 11);

4) the re-use of the first two bars, with a clumsy 'development' of the changing note pattern, weakly follows a bar which ends on a *tonic* chord (bar 12);

5) just when a good perfect cadence is needed to round the melody off, the unsatisfactory formula from bars 7 and 8 reappears, at the same moment as the *lowest* point of the melodic contour is reached!

Here is a second attempt at a completed version:

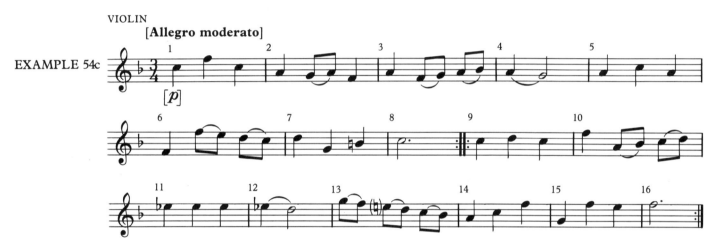

The general shape, flow and balance of phrases in this version are all much better, and the cadences are more convincing. There is a brief modulation implying the subdominant key in the second section. This delays the return to the tonic and makes for a more balanced structure.

This is what Bononcini wrote:

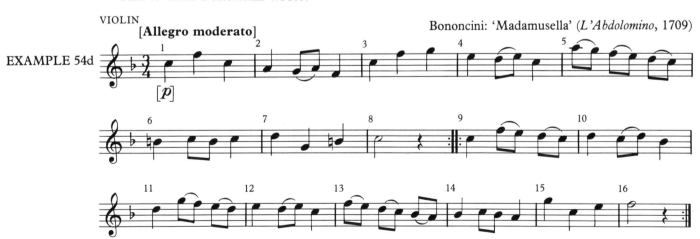

Comparing the three versions, consider how they are different and why Bononcini's melody, simple though it is, is easily the most effective.

On the next page are some examples of melodies from the Classical period. They all fall into the second of the three main categories described on p.36.

CLARINET (concert pitch)   Mozart: Clarinet Quintet (4th mvt)

EXAMPLE 55

*FLUTE   Mozart: Piano Sonata, K.331 (1st mvt)

EXAMPLE 56

OBOE   Mozart: Serenade for Wind, K.388 (4th mvt)

EXAMPLE 57

*Though this melody was originally for piano, it would be just as effective if played by another instrument, e.g. violin or oboe. It is included as a typical example of Classical melodic writing.

Each of the above melodies was composed as the 'theme' for a variation movement. The structures are consequently straightforward, both in key schemes and in the way the phrases and sections are balanced. Exs.55 & 56 are diatonic throughout; each melody introduces contrasted, though 'related', material for bars 9–12 and returns in bar 13 to the opening phrase in order to round off the theme. Note that bar 16 of Ex.56 is modified to allow for a 2-bar extension. A similar (but 4-bar) extension is seen in the second section of Ex.59, where the last phrase is repeated to make a more effective ending. Exs.57, 58 & 59 modulate briefly to the dominant at the mid-point. The comments made earlier in this Section (pp.37–43) about modulation in Baroque music apply on the whole to this kind of balanced Classical melody. You will see that only Ex.57 includes some variety of key (subdominant) in the second section. As already mentioned, asterisks have been used to mark appoggiaturas in Ex.55 and auxiliary notes in Ex.56.

The third main category of melodies will need only a few examples here, since they broadly follow the principles outlined above. Without the need for repeated sections, the structure can be still more flexible, though great care will be needed over the balance of the phrases, the preparation for modulation and cadencing, and the overall sense of unity of the melody.

Exs.60–63 below were composed as 16-bar melodies, although the first three examples divide into two 'halves' and into regular phrases.

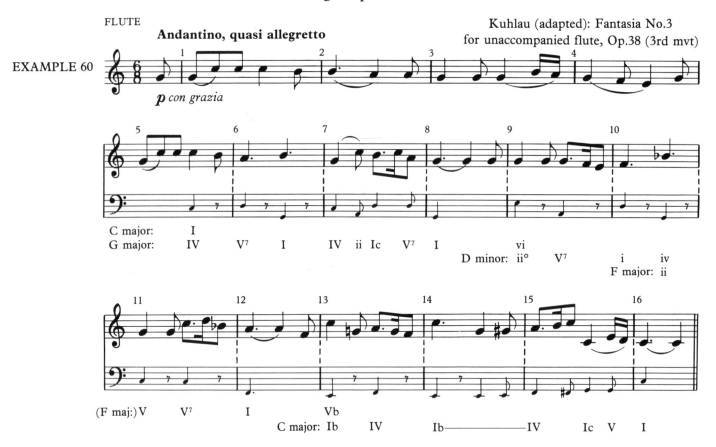

This melody, written by Kuhlau for unaccompanied flute, is in fact a version of a Serenade ('Deh vieni alla finestra') from Mozart's *Don Giovanni*. One or two small changes have been made to Kuhlau's version in order to make the harmony clearer. Notice that the second part touches on the key of D minor before moving into the subdominant. The G♯ in bar 14 and the bass clef F♯ in bar 15 are chromatic passing notes.

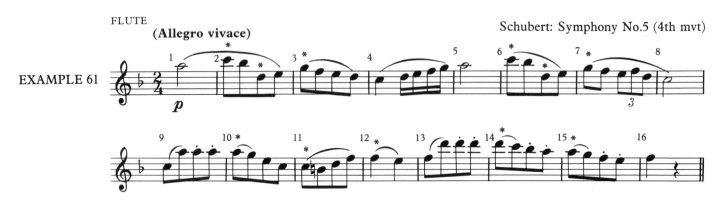

This melody is quoted in F major because it first appears in that key. The appoggiaturas (marked with asterisks) help to give the melody its forward impetus.

VIOLIN

Tempo di Valse   Tchaikovsky: Serenade for Strings (2nd mvt)

EXAMPLE 63

Two waltz tunes by Tchaikovsky show a well-planned overall shape and carefully balanced phrases. In Ex. 63 you will notice an interpolated section between the square brackets that are marked in bars 12 and 20. As with the Mozart Piano Sonata example in *AB Guide*, Part II, p. 185, the melody would fall into 4-bar phrases if the interpolated material were to be omitted. The process of sequential development, already a feature before bar 12, is continued and only broken at bar 18 after the highest note of the melody. Without ever modulating *into* the dominant, the interpolated section touches on that key; and rhythmic momentum is maintained right to the end. The artistic principle of 'variety with unity' is beautifully expressed in this flowing 23-bar melody.

The exercises that follow have been grouped in the three categories already explained. Where a transposing instrument has been required, the given opening is printed here *as the part would be written* for that instrument; i.e. the opening material is *not* at concert pitch, but already in the transposed key. Exercises 6d, 6h and 6n are examples of this method which is different from the layout in *Music Theory in Practice*, Grade 5, Section I. In writing your melodies try to remember:

1) to write in a style that will suit the given opening;

2) to keep within the compass of the given instrument and to write idiomatically, trying to imagine how the music will sound in performance;

3) to plan the structure of your melody, depending on what is asked (it can be helpful to sketch in the principal cadences and modulations before trying to write any part of your continuation – alterations or adjustments can be made later, if necessary);

4) to include non-harmony notes, which will help your melody to flow if they are suitable and well-placed;

5) to consider the harmonic implications of your melodic line;

6) to consider the overall shape, balance and direction of your completed melody;

7) to write in any necessary performance directions.

Exercise 4* Continue the following openings to make in each case a melodic composition of about 12 bars overall. The melody should be the first part of a movement in binary form and should end in the dominant.

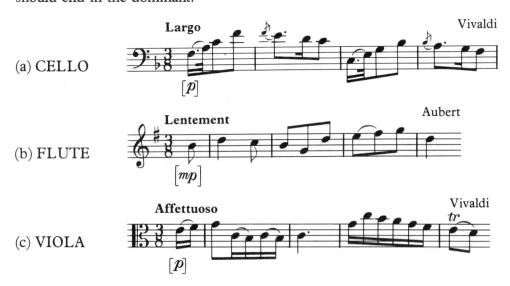

(a) CELLO

(b) FLUTE

(c) VIOLA

Continue the following openings to make in each case a melodic composition of about 16 bars overall. The melody should be the first part of a movement in binary form and should end in the dominant.

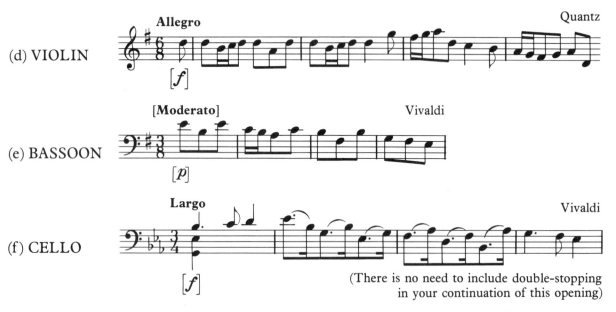

(d) VIOLIN

(e) BASSOON

(f) CELLO

(There is no need to include double-stopping in your continuation of this opening)

Continue the following openings to make in each case a melodic composition of about 16 bars overall. The melody should modulate as shown and should be a complete movement in binary form, ending in the tonic.

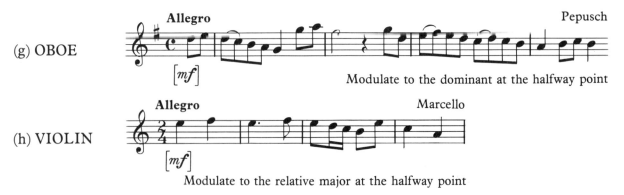

(g) OBOE

Modulate to the dominant at the halfway point

(h) VIOLIN

Modulate to the relative major at the halfway point

*For Exercises 4–7, students should use their own manuscript paper.

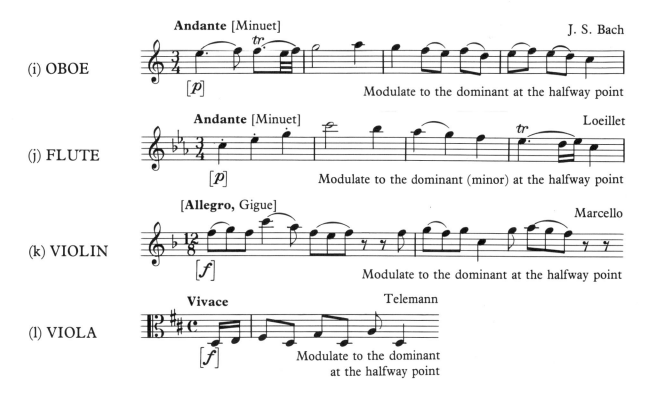

Exercise 5 Continue the following openings to make in each case a balanced melodic composition of about 16 bars. Modulate as shown at the halfway point and end in the tonic.

Exercise 5 (cont.)

(g) BASSOON

(h) VIOLIN

Exercise 6 Continue the following openings to make in each case a melodic composition of between 14 and 20 bars. Make a principal modulation as shown and end in the tonic. Passing modulations to other keys may be included if you wish.

(a) VIOLIN

(b) VIOLA

(c) CELLO

(d) CLARINET in B♭

(e) VIOLIN

(f) FLUTE

(g) FLUTE

Melodic composition in more modern styles

Throughout the Baroque and Classical periods and for most of the 19th century, melody was closely related to harmony. Melodic patterns frequently followed chord shapes (see *AB Guide*, Part II, 18/2), and melodies grew out of their underlying harmonies – the chord progressions which define the tonality of the music and any subsidiary keys which may be used.

During the 20th century many composers have continued to write tonally and have shaped their melodies from traditional harmonic progressions. Other composers have been more adventurous and have explored new ways of using familiar chords or have added 'foreign' notes to simple diatonic chords to give spice to the harmony. There have also been composers who have tried to free themselves from the old system of keys and key relationships by turning to folk music, with its modal melodies, or inventing new modes and scales. These and other modern developments are described in *AB Guide*, Part II, Chapter 24.

The various routes away from the tonal system all led towards a new approach to composition in which harmony was no longer the principal controlling factor. This may be one reason why so many composers in the 20th century have written monophonic pieces (i.e. pieces for a solo voice or instrument without accompaniment). One of the best-known examples from the early part of the century is Debussy's *Syrinx* for unaccompanied flute; it was composed in 1913 as incidental music for the scene of the death of Pan ('syrinx' is another word for 'panpipes') in a play by Gabriel Mourey, but was not published until 1927. Here is the opening paragraph:

EXAMPLE 64

As you can see, the music is written with a key signature of five flats. This is the key signature for B♭ minor, and since the passage begins and ends on B♭ it looks at first glance as though the music is in that key. But when the passage is played it does not sound as though it is in B♭ minor, or indeed in any other key. No key-centre is ever defined because there are no perfect cadences, and the melodic patterns are not built out of conventional chord progressions. Nevertheless, the pattern produced by the different pitches is perfectly coherent, so there must be some other basis for the melodic construction. We shall examine what that basis is in a moment, but before doing so let us consider the rhythmic organisation of the passage.

The melodies discussed in the earlier part of this Section all have a strong sense of metrical pulse. Here, Debussy establishes a slow, triple-time pulse in the first bar but then abandons it by inserting a pause and a comma in bar 2. The pulse is re-established in bar 3, but the great range of note values (from ♪ to 𝅗𝅥 𝅘𝅥) and the commas in bars 4 and 5 make it difficult to detect any underlying pattern of regular stressed and unstressed beats. As a result of this rhythmic freedom and lack of a key-centre, the music sounds like an improvised cadenza, yet there is nothing random about its construction. The first phrase (bars 1–2) consists of a decorated falling figure which then returns to its starting-point by leaping up a major 6th from D♭ to B♭. This makes B♭ the most important note in the first phrase, but it does not sound like a tonic. It is merely a temporary resting-place before the second phrase extends the opening idea, restating the first bar and then changing direction so that the melody begins to rise. At the end of bar 4 it tucks back again in preparation for an arpeggio figure at the end of bar 5, which sweeps up through an octave to take the melody towards its highest point, the E♭ in bar 8 which then falls back to B♭.

Despite the varied rhythmic patterns and the absence of conventional cadences, certain notes sound more important than others because they are stressed, or are repeated, or are the highest or lowest points of a phrase, or are approached by leap. The principal melody notes of the first phrase give the outline shown in Ex.65a, while those from the beginning of bar 4 to the comma in bar 5 can be outlined as shown in Ex.65b.

EXAMPLE 65a  EXAMPLE 65b

If all these notes are set out next to each other, they produce the following scale:

EXAMPLE 66

As you can see, the scale consists of two cells, one made up of three whole-tone steps (T), the other of three semitones (ST). The two cells are separated from each other by an augmented 2nd (E♮ to D♭). Since the first cell is heard only in its descending form and the second only as an ascending figure, the scale is a purely theoretical arrangement of the notes. The character of the music derives from its melodic shapes: it is modal. However, the melodic shapes do not correspond with any of the traditional modes (Dorian, Phrygian etc.) used in Western music. The mode is one which Debussy himself has invented.

Notice that Debussy does not confine himself to the notes of this modal scale, but decorates the main melody notes with others which loop around or pass between the principal pitches. Notice, too, that the highest note in the passage, the E♭ in bar 8, is not present in the scale. Its appearance at the cadence introduces a new colour to the music in preparation for development of the opening material. If Debussy had wanted the piece to finish at this point, he would have found another way of ending it. In fact, he continues for a further 27 bars, varying the mode, introducing pentatonic patterns and ending with a whole-tone scale. If possible, listen to a recording of the work. You will be struck by the importance of tone colour (the piece would sound very different if played on violin or clarinet) and by the way in which the melodic and rhythmic shapes make a coherent pattern despite the absence of a key-centre and lack of a sustained metrical pulse.

A great deal of 20th-century music is like *Syrinx* in breaking away from the domination of the bar-line and established ideas about key-notes and key relationships. Debussy himself once said that discipline must be sought in freedom, not in formulas. The idea that composers are free to do what they like can give the impression that to compose in a modern idiom is very easy. In fact, composers who have abandoned the principles of tonal harmony have needed to look for other ways of making their music coherent. A piece of music in which the pitches are chosen at random and put together in a totally unorganised way will have no intelligible shape; it will just be noise. Music, unlike noise, is the result of *planned* use of sounds, ordered and controlled to make a logical progression. This is as true of music which consists of a single melodic line as it is of music for a combination of instruments and/or voices.

One way of imposing order on music which is not tonal is to confine the material to just a few notes and then explore their intervallic relationships. Varèse does this in *Density 21.5*, also for unaccompanied flute. It was composed in 1936 for Georges Barrère as an inauguration piece for his platinum flute[1] and revised ten years later. Here is the opening section:

EXAMPLE 67

© Property of G. Ricordi C.s.p.a.
Reprinted by permission

The material here could hardly be simpler. The piece begins with a tiny rhythmic figure ( ) in which the first two notes sound like a decoration of the third long note, F♯. The rhythmic figure is repeated at the end of bar 3 (though this time the third note is considerably shorter) and so establishes itself as a motif. There is an expectation that it will be heard again; and indeed it is in bars 9 and 15, and also, in modified form, in bar 4. Repetitions of the motif provide the listener with reference points: the rhythmic pattern, which occurs at the beginning of each of the four principal phrases, is instantly recognisable even though the pitches are eventually transposed.

Using this rhythmic figure as his starting-point, Varèse goes on to construct a melodic line which moves no more than a minor 3rd either side of E in the first two phrases but then rises through more than two octaves from low C♯ at the beginning of bar 6 to high G at the end of the extract. Notice that only five pitches – F, E, F♯, C♯ and G – are used in the first five bars. The way in which these pitches are arranged into melodic and rhythmic patterns is such that two intervals are established as particularly important: the perfect 4th (bar 2) and the diminished 5th, first heard in bar 2 and repeated in bars 4 and 5. The chromatic wriggle at the beginning (F – E – F♯) provides two more intervals – semitone and tone – for subsequent exploration; while a further interval, the minor 3rd, is introduced in bar 5. Apart from the octave jump in bar 13, these are the only intervals used

---

[1]Platinum is an extremely heavy metal, with a density, or mass per unit volume, of 21.5 grams per cubic centimetre. This accounts for the somewhat strange title of the work.

throughout the entire extract, though they are sometimes spelt differently: the diminished 5th appears as an augmented 4th in bars 11, 12 and 13, while the major 2nd is notated as a diminished 3rd in bar 15.

Exclusive use of these five intervals and repetitions of the rhythmic motif are the means by which Varèse unifies this first paragraph of his composition. The basic material is extremely simple, yet even after repeated hearings it is difficult for the listener to remember the melody in any detail. This is partly because the music has no tonal, or even modal, basis and partly because the melodic patterns do not follow familiar chord shapes. But the principal reason why the melody is so difficult to remember is that the rhythmic organisation is irregular. The music is in ¢ ($\frac{4}{4}$) time, but there is little feeling of metrical pulse because the frequent displacement of accents has the effect of cancelling the bar-line. Furthermore, no two bars have exactly the same rhythmic pattern: the only rhythmic figure heard more than once is the unifying motif , the third note of which is in any case of different length each time the figure is used. The impression given by the music is of incantatory figures which are constantly being modified yet seem to change very slowly. Notice, for example, how the melodic and rhythmic patterns of the first phrase (bars 1–3) are modified in bars 3–5 without any new pitches being introduced. Notice, too, how the wriggling chromatic figure in bar 1 is stretched out over more than two bars when it appears a minor 6th higher (bars 9–11).

Two other features of this extract should be noted. The first is the way in which Varèse uses a very wide dynamic range (from quieter than p to fff) and gives very detailed dynamic directions. The second feature is the contour of the melody, which has some very wide leaps towards the end of the extract. In bar 12, the falling perfect 4th (derived from the rising perfect 4th in bar 2) is displaced by an octave, becoming a perfect 11th. There are further octave displacements in bars 13 and 16, where the minor 2nd becomes a minor 9th; and at the end of the extract the minor 2nd is displaced by two octaves, producing the widest interval of all. These abrupt shifts of register, like the sudden contrasts in dynamic level, are used for colouristic effect.

Interest in colouristic devices is very common among 20th-century composers whose music no longer relies on the old system of keys and key relationships. Composers who have abandoned tonal principles (as well as many composers who have continued to write tonally) have tended to place considerable emphasis on the *quality* of sound, or **timbre**. This has led them to give very detailed directions for dynamics, phrasing and articulation, and to explore new ways of using instruments, often exploiting the extremes of an instrument's compass. Wide leaps are frequently used for colouristic purposes, as in *Density 21.5*, but sometimes composers use octave displacements simply to give character to a melody. An example of this can be seen in the second movement of Stravinsky's *Symphony of Psalms*. The movement begins with a melody played by solo oboe. This melody, which is later developed fugally, could have been written like this:

EXAMPLE 68a

Instead Stravinsky transposes certain notes into the higher octave, so making the melodic shape much more interesting and memorable:

EXAMPLE 68b

The contour of this melody is one of the things that make it sound like a product of the 20th century rather than of some earlier period. Another is the rhythmic organisation. In bar 2, ties to the D and B♮ shift the accents to weak beats: these syncopations add considerably to the interest. Notice that Stravinsky writes phrase marks across the beat, not only in bar 2 but also in bars 3 and 4 where the rhythm is not otherwise syncopated. These phrase marks produce a variety of rhythmic patterns which the listener hears in relation to the slow, quadruple-time pulse established in bar 1.

The three examples of non-traditional melodic writing we have looked at so far are all from the first half of the 20th century. In each of them, variety is achieved, and interest sustained, by simple modification of the initial material. Beginners often make the mistake of introducing too much variety into their music. Instead of looking for ways in which the opening material can be developed, they come up with a series of contrasted ideas which bear little relationship to each other or to the opening. In *Density 21.5* Varèse constructs a complete musical paragraph from five basic intervals. This piece is an excellent example of how a great deal can be made from very little.

Let us turn next to a piece for solo horn by Benjamin Britten – the Prologue to his *Serenade* for tenor, horn and strings, composed in 1943. Here, the composer restricts his material to the notes of the harmonic series, directing the performer to play the whole piece on natural harmonics (i.e. not to produce any note by use of valves). The pitches available are the first twelve harmonics above the fundamental C (sounding F, a 5th below the written note).

EXAMPLE 69

Selecting only from these pitches, three of which he does not use at all, Britten constructs a perfect miniature in which fluctuations of tempo, metre and dynamics are as important as the melodic shapes. Notice that there is no time signature. The metre is irregular and, rather than writing numerous changes of time signature, Britten dispenses with it altogether. This is not unusual in 20th-century music. Where the metre is very irregular, composers sometimes do not even write bar-lines, especially if they intend the pulse to be flexible.

EXAMPLE 70

This horn solo, like the flute piece by Varèse, achieves its variety through contrasts in tone colour, dynamics and rhythm rather than through contrasts of thematic material.

However, there are pieces in which the opening thematic idea is so terse that a second, complementary idea is needed. An example of this can be seen in the first movement of Richard Rodney Bennett's Sonatina for solo clarinet (1981). Here are the first 20 bars:

EXAMPLE 71

© Novello & Co. Ltd
Reprinted by permission

The first phrase is extremely brief – an arpeggio which rises rapidly in even quavers from low E to high C♯. The complementary phrase (bars 2–4) repeats the C♯, which is held for five quaver beats, and then moves down by steps of a tone and semitone before the arpeggio figure is resumed, this time falling. Repeated notes and stepwise movement are integrated with the arpeggio figures throughout the first ten bars of the movement. Without this contrasted idea, which is subjected to more radical modification from bar 11 onwards, the music would consist entirely of rising and falling arpeggios and would soon become tiresome. Music needs repetition and unity, but it also needs variety. It is by balancing variety with unifying repetitions that composers build coherent and interesting structures.

You will notice that the arpeggio figures in this extract are based on familiar chord shapes: they are all triads, most of them appearing in second inversion (i.e. as $\frac{6}{4}$ chords). The three chords used in bar 1 are built on notes a semitone apart. Transposed into the same octave they are these:

EXAMPLE 72

Similarly, the bass notes (and therefore also the roots) of the two $\frac{6}{4}$ chords in bar 3 are also a semitone apart, while the first three chords in bars 5–6 have bass notes and roots a tone apart. These chord progressions do not establish a tonic with its own dominant and leading note, so the music is not in any particular key. This does not mean that all the pitches are equally important. In the first ten bars, one note – C♯, written enharmonically as D♭ in bar 7 – is given prominence, while the most important note from bar 11 onwards is E. Since neither of these notes can be described as a tonic, another term is needed. In 20th-century music which is outside the old tonal system, such notes are usually called 'pitch-centres'. Notice that there is no key signature. Where a functional key does not exist, key signatures are not normally used.

Another piece which derives an important part of its material from a recognisable chord shape is the second movement of Britten's First Suite for unaccompanied cello, composed in 1964. This movement, entitled 'Lamento' (meaning 'Lament'), has a simple binary structure. Here is the first section:

CELLO

EXAMPLE 73

©1966 Faber Music Ltd
Reprinted by permission

At first glance, this music seems to be in E minor. It has a key signature of one sharp, and the extract ends with an arpeggiated E minor triad. If you examine the passage more closely, you will see that the melody consists of five phrases, each ending with an E minor arpeggio, plus a short final phrase (bar 6) which repeats the E minor triad with the rhythm slightly altered. It is easy to identify the phrase lengths: they are marked off by the bar-lines which are drawn for this very purpose and have no other significance. Note that the slurs indicate bowings, not phrase lengths.

Everything that has been said about this piece so far seems to confirm that the music is indeed in E minor. However, if you play the first phrase you will discover that another key is suggested before the E minor arpeggio occurs. The first four notes sound as though they are in E *flat* minor: if the first note (F♯) were written enharmonically as G♭ you would be able to see as well as hear that the music begins with a strong implication of that key. The first phrase thus establishes two tonal centres a semitone apart from each other.

This conflict is present throughout the extract. Each of the next four phrases steers its way towards E♭ before cadencing in E minor. The expressive power of the music derives from the tension between these two tonal centres, a tension which is increased as the phrase lengths expand and then contract. This passage provides another example of how a complete paragraph can be developed from the ideas contained in the opening phrase.

The openings in the examination papers will all contain at least one feature susceptible of development; some of the openings will provide enough material for simple modification and extension on lines similar to the examples discussed above. At Grade 6, knowledge of the more 'advanced' styles and techniques practised by 20th-century composers is not required. However, you will be expected to show an understanding of more traditional 20th-century styles. You should therefore listen to as many examples as you can, armed whenever possible with a score so you can see how the sounds are notated. Do not confine your listening and score study to monophonic pieces. You will learn a great deal about melodic construction and the way instruments are used by studying orchestral works and other ensemble pieces.

When considering how a given opening might be continued, look at the rhythm as well as the melodic shape, taking account of any rests. Silences are just as important as the sounds either side of them and can be an essential part of the rhythmic design. Look back at Ex. 71 where the rests are an important part of the musical conception, especially towards the end of the extract, and compare it with Ex. 73 which is a continuously flowing melody, unbroken by any rests until the last bar. Before beginning to write your continuation, look at the style and/or tempo indications and take into account any marks of phrasing and articulation. Notice the dynamic markings. Are there sudden contrasts of loud and soft sounds, or is the whole of the opening at one dynamic level? All these things will help you to establish the character of the opening and decide how it might go on. You will usually be asked to compose a complete piece of about 16 bars, but sometimes you may be asked to continue a given opening to make the first section of a longer composition. Whichever request is made, your melody should be a self-contained musical paragraph which can stand on its own.

Your melodies will be judged on their effectiveness as music. You must write in a style that suits the instrument and you will be expected to give appropriately detailed directions for phrasing, articulation and dynamics. *Above all, your continuation must be consistent with the given opening.* This point cannot be stressed too strongly. It would not be the slightest use to go into the examination room with a prepared 'continuation' which you have memorised and intend to attach to the given opening, whatever that opening might be!

Exercise 7 Continue the following openings to make in each case a self-contained musical paragraph of between 14 and 20 bars. The paragraph may be a complete composition or the first section of a longer composition. Add marks of expression, phrasing (including bowing, where appropriate) and articulation.

(a) VIOLA

(b) BASSOON

(c) FLUTE

(d) CELLO

D General Exercises

In the examination you will have to answer questions on TWO extracts, one of which will be from music for one, two or possibly three performers; the other extract will be from an open score of music for a minimum of four performers up to full orchestra with voices. The number of questions will vary from examination to examination depending upon the scope of the extract, the difficulty of the questions and the amount of time you will need to write your answers; the examples on the next few pages will give you an idea of the range and style of the questions to expect and guide you as to the depth of study required.

You should make frequent reference to *The AB Guide to Music Theory*, Parts I & II, as well as to other books when preparing your answers. Although the range of music from which extracts could be taken is unlimited, it will be seen that the questions set under this section are part of a steady progression in difficulty from Grade 5 to Grade 8, and that they relate specifically to the Grade 6 syllabus. No further list of performance directions and other terms is provided, though greater knowledge (at least of standard terms in Italian, French and German) will be expected than for Grade 5. In general, the more music you have studied from the printed page and open score the better equipped you will be to answer questions under this section.

You will be asked to identify and describe individual chords in some of the extracts. You may describe these chords by using any of the methods outlined in *The AB Guide to Music Theory*, Parts I & II, provided you are clear and complete in your description. However, the use of Extended Roman numeral notation is the preferred method of describing chords from Grade 6 onwards; correct use of the symbols provides an unambiguous description both of the chord and of its function within the key in which it appears. A full description of the method will be found in *The AB Guide to Music Theory*, Part II, Appendix D; Section B of this publication (pages 24–5) gives further explanations and examples. You will see that in some of the exercises below a bracket (⌐‾‾‾‾⌐) is drawn where one of the chords is to be identified; *all* the harmony notes within the bracket are to be included but only one chord description is required (see Exercises 8–10).

Exercise 8 Study this extract and then answer the questions below.

(a) For which of the following instruments do you think the music was written:

piano, harp, harpsichord, xylophone, celeste? ....

(b) Complete the following statements:

    (i)   The music begins in the key of .... but has modulated to the key of

           .... by the end of the extract.

    (ii)   The interval between the first two notes of the piece (i.e. a *rising* perfect 4th)

           reappears .... times later.

(c) In bar 7 the musical material for the first two beats is re-used in a slightly modified form for the last two beats. Which of the following terms best describes the process:

fugue, inversion, canon, imitation, sequence? ....

(d) Write out the right-hand part in bar 9, first two beats, as it might be played.

(e) Identify the chords marked 1–6 by writing on the dotted lines below. Use either appropriate symbols or verbal description. Indicate any inversions and show whether the chords are major, minor, augmented or diminished.

    1 ....   2 ....

    3 ....   4 ....

    5 ....   6 ....

(f) Draw a circle round each non-harmony note in bar 5.

(g) Who of the following is the most likely composer of this piece:

Handel, Schubert, Tchaikovsky, Debussy, Vaughan Williams? ....

Exercise 9   Study this extract and then answer the questions below.

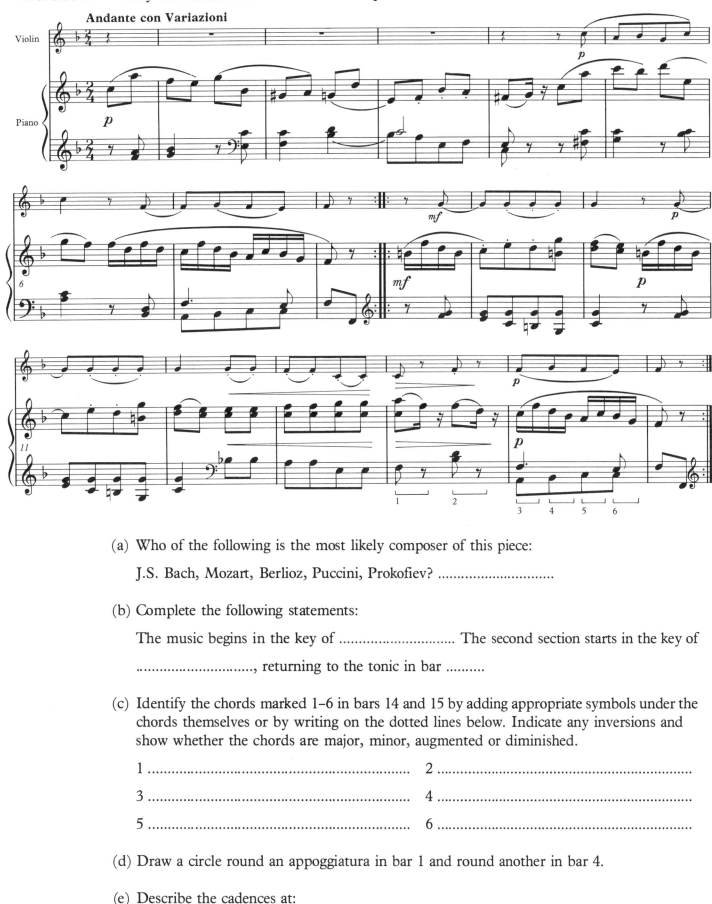

(a) Who of the following is the most likely composer of this piece:

   J.S. Bach, Mozart, Berlioz, Puccini, Prokofiev? ....

(b) Complete the following statements:

   The music begins in the key of .... The second section starts in the key of

   ...., returning to the tonic in bar ....

(c) Identify the chords marked 1–6 in bars 14 and 15 by adding appropriate symbols under the chords themselves or by writing on the dotted lines below. Indicate any inversions and show whether the chords are major, minor, augmented or diminished.

   1 ....   2 ....

   3 ....   4 ....

   5 ....   6 ....

(d) Draw a circle round an appoggiatura in bar 1 and round another in bar 4.

(e) Describe the cadences at:

   (i)   last quaver bar 3 to first crotchet bar 4 ....

   (ii)   last quaver bar 11 to first crotchet bar 12 ....

(f) Add phrase marks above the violin part to show the phrase structure of the extract.

Exercise 10   Study this extract and then answer the questions below.

(a) Who of the following is the most likely composer of this piece:

Scarlatti, Beethoven, Chopin, Stravinsky? ....

(b) Explain each of the following:

Lento ....   *P* ⌐_____⌐ ....

rubato ....   *sf* (bar 17) ....

(c) (i)   What is the key of the first four bars? ....

(ii)   Identify the chords marked 1–3 by adding appropriate symbols under the chords themselves or by writing on the dotted lines below. Indicate any inversions and show whether the chords are major, minor, augmented or diminished.

1 ....   2 ....

3 ....

(d) (i)   The music moves into a new key for bars 17–20. What is the new key? ....

(ii)   Name the cadence in bars 19–20. ....

(e) Draw a circle round: (i) an acciaccatura; (ii) a passing note.

(f) Which of the following titles is most appropriate for the piece:

Prelude, Mazurka, Tango, Nocturne, Gigue? ....

Exercise 11 Study this piano piece by Bartók and then answer the questions below.

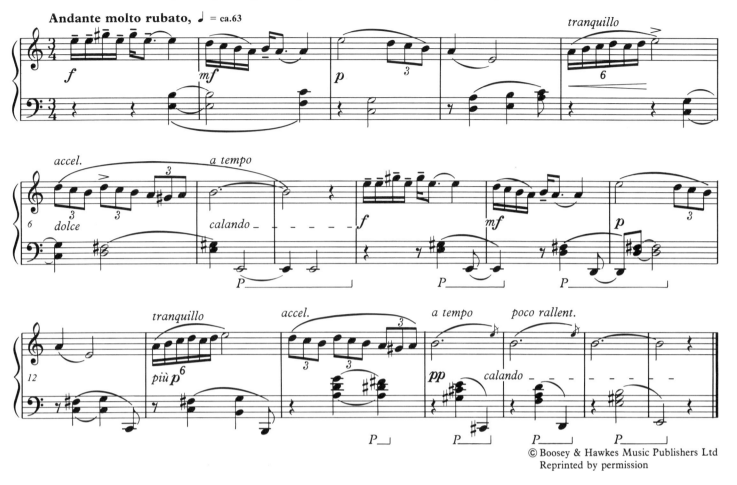

(a) In the following list of musical genres underline those to which Bartók contributed:

opera, sacred oratorio, string quartet, ballet music, trumpet concerto, piano concerto.

(b) Explain each of the following:

♩ = ca. 63 ....

accel. (bar 6) ....

dolce (bar 6) ....

calando (bar 7) ....

(c) Which is the *first* bar in the left-hand part to show the use of syncopation? Bar ....

(d) Answer TRUE or UNTRUE to each of the following statements:

(i) The piece is designed to produce an expressive and sonorous effect. ....

(ii) Although notated in simple triple time, the piece is really in compound time. ....

(iii) The piece is in ternary form. ....

(e) At one place in the piece the composer writes a full major triad, the notes of which are to be played at the same moment. Name the bar in which this occurs. Bar ....

(f) Which of the following titles best suits this piece:

Viennese Waltz, Peasant's Flute,
Trumpet Tune, Lady Farnaby's Jig? ....

Exercise 12   Study the extract opposite and then answer the questions below.

(a) Who of the following is the most likely composer of the extract:

Handel, Haydn, Schubert, Borodin, Schoenberg? ....

(b) Explain each of the following:

Corno in F   ....

div. (bar 5)   ....

espr. cantabile ....

⋮ (bar 5)   ....

(c) Write out the Corno in F part for bars 5 and 6 at concert pitch, using the appropriate key signature.

(d) (i)   Name the key of this extract. ....

(ii)   The accompaniment is derived from diatonic chords and their inversions; *one* chord only

is a minor chord in root position. In which bar does this occur? Bar ....

(e) Answer TRUE or UNTRUE to each of the following statements:

(i)   The principal melody begins immediately. ....

(ii)   The harp part adds both background harmony and colour. ....

(iii) The rich string writing will make the harp part from bar 5 onwards difficult to hear.

....

(f) Name the interval formed by the two viola parts on the *first* beat of each of the following bars:

(i)   Bar 6 ....   (ii) Bar 7 ....

(iii) Bar 8..................................   (iv) Bar 9 ....

Exercise 13   Study the extract opposite from Beethoven's Symphony No.8 in F, and then answer the questions below.

(a) (i)   What is the time signature? ....

(ii)   Complete the following statements:

The movement is in F major, but at the beginning of this extract there is a

modulation to the key of .... The key of F major returns in bar ....

(iii)   Draw a circle round the bass note of a dominant 7th chord.

(b) Explain the meaning of the following:

dolce (bar 234)   ....   arco (bar 249) ....

ritard. (bar 240) ....   *sf* (bar 257)   ....

1 (bar 234)   ....

(c) (i)   What abbreviations are used here for these instruments?

horns ....   double basses ....   clarinets ....   bassoons ....

(ii)   In which key are the clarinets pitched? They are clarinets in ....

(iii)   Beethoven is using horns in F. What note do they sound in the last bar? ....

(iv)   What instrument in the extract, other than clarinets and horns, sounds at

a different pitch to that written? .... What is the interval between

its sound and its written note? ....

(d) Write out bar 250 of the viola part as it is played.

(e) Complete the following statement:

In bars 243–4 the .... is playing the melody .... octaves below the ....

(f) (i)   What percussion instrument is used? ....

(ii)   In which bar does it enter? ....

(iii)   Why do you think it does not play in bar 257 (the last bar)?

....

....

....

Exercise 14 Study the extract opposite from Britten's *A Boy was Born* and then answer the questions below.

(a) From which of the following kinds of music is the extract most likely to have been taken: madrigal, motet, choral symphony, cantata, verse anthem? ....

(b) Explain each of the following:

Gt. to Ped. (bar 1) ....

Un poco più lento (bar 16) ....

Semichorus tacet (bar 22) ....

Attacca (bar 23) ....

(c) Write out the voice parts in bars 2–7 (inclusive) in short score.

(d) Explain why the composer has written '(B♭)' above the soprano part and '(E♭)' above the alto part in bar 18.

....

....

(e) Locate TWO examples of syncopation in the tenor and bass parts, giving the bar numbers in which the examples occur. Bar .... and bar ....

(f) Comment on the vocal part-writing in bars 2 and 3.

....

....

(g) Give the titles of ONE work by Britten in each of the following categories:

Chorus and orchestra ....

Solo voice and instrumental ensemble ....

Opera ....

Exercise 15   Study this extract and then answer the questions below.

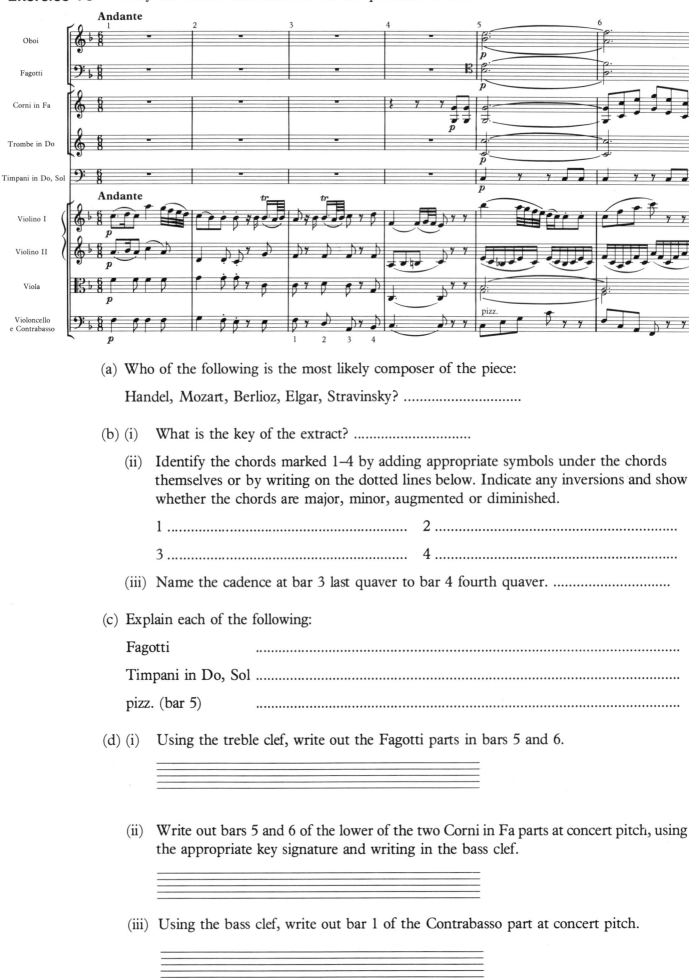

(a) Who of the following is the most likely composer of the piece:

Handel, Mozart, Berlioz, Elgar, Stravinsky? ....

(b) (i)   What is the key of the extract? ....

   (ii)   Identify the chords marked 1–4 by adding appropriate symbols under the chords
          themselves or by writing on the dotted lines below. Indicate any inversions and show
          whether the chords are major, minor, augmented or diminished.

   1 ....   2 ....

   3 ....   4 ....

   (iii) Name the cadence at bar 3 last quaver to bar 4 fourth quaver. ....

(c) Explain each of the following:

   Fagotti   ....

   Timpani in Do, Sol ....

   pizz. (bar 5)   ....

(d) (i)   Using the treble clef, write out the Fagotti parts in bars 5 and 6.

   (ii)   Write out bars 5 and 6 of the lower of the two Corni in Fa parts at concert pitch, using
          the appropriate key signature and writing in the bass clef.

   (iii) Using the bass clef, write out bar 1 of the Contrabasso part at concert pitch.

(e) Draw a circle round each of the non-harmony notes in bar 5.